Astrotourism

Astrotourism

Star Gazers, Eclipse Chasers, and the Dark Sky Movement

Michael Marlin

BUSINESS EXPERT PRESS
Leader in applied, concise business books

Astrotourism: Star Gazers, Eclipse Chasers, and the Dark Sky Movement

Edited by Cindy Hartman

Cover design by G.Brad Lewis/volcanoman.com

Interior design by Exeter Premedia Services Private Ltd., Chennai, India

First published in 2021 by
Business Expert Press, LLC
222 East 46th Street, New York, NY 10017
www.businessexpertpress.com

ISBN-13: 978-1-63742-066-9 (paperback)
ISBN-13: 978-1-63742-067-6 (e-book)

Business Expert Press Tourism and Hospitality Management Collection

Collection ISSN: 2375-9623 (print)
Collection ISSN: 2375-9631 (electronic)

First edition: 2021

10 9 8 7 6 5 4 3 2 1

This book is dedicated to the committed champions of our dark skies, whose gaze of conviction goes past the horizon. Their actions protect and preserve one of our planet's remarkable features, its view of eternity and the sparkling stars that lure us there.

Description

In the span of a single lifetime, light pollution from Artificial Light At Night (ALAN) has severed our connection with the stars that we've had since the dawn of time. With the nocturnal biosphere significantly altered, light's anthropogenic influence has compelled millions of people to seek out the last remaining dark skies.

This book explores the growth of the astrotourism, identifies star seeker trends, how the stars have shaped civilizations, and the budding space tourism industry. Learn ways to develop a destination, find customers, and our relationship with the night sky. Meteor storms, eclipses, auroras, and other celestial phenomena have lured travelers for years and here the author expands the field of astrotourism with the inclusion of astronomical clocks, megaliths, and sundials, which track the movement of the stars.

Keywords

astrotourism; space tourism; tourism; astronomy; astronomy tourism; astronomical; eco-tourism; green tourism; sustainable tourism; star gazing; eclipse chasing; star tourism; dark sky; astrotourist; solar eclipse; aurora borealis; constellations; ALAN; artificial light at night; light pollution; skyglow; meteors; full moon; 2024 eclipse; Great America Eclipse

Contents

Preface

It was a clear Hawaiian night, and it was possible to walk up to the very edge of an active lava flow on the slopes of Kilauea—the blood of the earth exposed to the air, its intense heat briefly glowing then rapidly cooling to become dark stone. People would ask me, "How close can you get?" My response was always, "How far can you put your head into an oven?" Watching people transfixed by the light in the dark, it dawned on me that all life is drawn to light and the whole world would want to see a show about that. That thought was a pivotal moment in my history.

A few years earlier, I had quit a 15-year career as a highly successful stage performer. I had pioneered a genre, becoming the first comedy talking juggler in the history of Las Vegas. A video of me can still be found on YouTube, doing my shtick on Don Kirshner's Rock Concert in 1977. I appeared on national TV in the U.S. and across Europe, performed with ballet companies and orchestras, headlined comedy clubs, filling every bucket available for a juggler. You are only as old as your act—and I didn't want to grow old doing my act—so I left my career, society, and civilization. I ended up in the jungles of the Big Island in Hawaii, where I built and lived in a treehouse without electricity for five years.

After the glaring lights of LA and Las Vegas, the darkness of night was soothing to my soul. It was on these Hawaiian nights, the stars sweeping overhead from one horizon to the other, that I felt connected to something more eternal than my name on a marquee for a week. It was in this darkness, my face hot from the lava, that a seed was planted for the sapling of a new idea. The tree I had been living in had served its purpose, and it was time for me to come down out of it.

I returned to civilization and the performing arts to raise awareness of the loss of our night skies due to light pollution. Entertainment spreads faster and is consumed more enthusiastically than educational programs and with this in mind, I created a show that was performed in a darkened theater, with unseen performers creating moving tapestries of light and color. My goal was to create the same sense of wonder I felt when looking at a night sky.

My brainchild, LUMA: Theater of Light and Art in Darkness, performed across generations and around the world. In 1987, light pollution was a fringe topic that was not on peoples' radar. Thirty-plus years later, light pollution has become a driver in the travel market. It is time for those who still live under a starry night sky to learn how to capture the imagination of travelers, lovers of the night, and what we now call, astrotourists.

My journey has come full circle, and rather than inviting people into a theater, this book is an invitation to journey out into the evening's shadow to experience the awe, amazement, and majesty that is everybody's birthright: a view of the heavens. A dark sky is a free resource that needs little to capitalize on. If you are a tour guide, hotelier, outfitter, resort manager, or anyone whose place of business or residence can be found under a dark sky—and you do not take advantage—then, "The fault....lies not within the stars, but in ourselves."

Foreword

Early April in Alaska is barely beyond winter, yet I stood patiently with my father and a group of other avid astronomers, waiting to look through the telescope eyepiece at the dusty streak of a comet passing through our solar system. It was 1997, and the comet Hale-Bopp was near its closest point to the sun and earth on its 2,533-year orbit. Seeing Hale-Bopp was my first and earliest memory of discovering the wonders of the night sky; I've since been fortunate to build a career focused on experiencing astronomy first-hand and sharing my experiences as a resource for others. But for most of my career, I wasn't aware that there was a formal name for the type of tourism I was participating in and promoting—astrotourism— and it dates back to almost the beginning of civilization.

For the entirety of human history, our lives have been shaped by astronomical phenomena. This has both a biological basis and a cultural one; for this reason we have strong evidence about the power of light to affect human sleep/wake cycles as well as millennia-old monuments which mark the dance of the moon and sun across the sky throughout each year. Despite the fact that groups of humans warmed themselves around a fire each night to keep the darkness and cold at bay, it has only been in the last two centuries that our capabilities have truly managed to push the night away.

Artificial light at night (ALAN) is one of the great plagues of the 21st century, though many people might not know about it—or even understand how it impacts us. This is demonstrated poignantly in an anecdote within these pages about the power of seeing the night sky demonstrated through the film *Soylent Green*. We're missing something due to ALAN, but we don't even know what we're missing until we see the pristine night sky above us, awash in starlight and moonlight.

Thanks to the double-edged sword of the ubiquity of media on the internet, the tide is slowly changing, as more people travel to seek out the night sky, share their experience, and become ambassadors for its protection. For every beautiful Milky Way photo we see posted on Instagram, there are thousands of users who are exposed and begin to wonder how they can see the same with their own eyes. The concept of astrotourism—traveling to experience the wonder of the night sky or learn more about astronomy and space science—is spreading, and represents an opportunity for destinations and businesses that can serve that interest.

To that end, *Astrotourism: Star Gazers, Eclipse Chasers and the Astronomical Rise of the Dark Sky Movement* presents an invaluable resource to those in the astrotourism industry (whether they are aware of being in the industry or not). Certainly operators offering night sky tours and destinations which have (or are near) locales that have received dark sky designation status are actively and avidly courting astrotourists and the financial impact they bring to local economies. But many more opportunities still exist for businesses and destinations that are as yet unaware of the power of the astrotourist dollar to improve a natural resource we all take for granted, the night sky.

Within these pages you'll discover a plethora of information and resources to help first educate and then inspire you to partake in the astrotourism niche of the tourism and hospitality industry. Your mind will be opened to the wide range of experiences which can be classified as and appeal to prospective astrotourists—even those in large urban areas. You'll also learn about the astronomical phenomena that take place overhead each night (and day) that can draw tourists to specific destinations, regions, or experiences. Many of these represent economic opportunities which cannot be overstated: hundreds of thousands—if not millions—of people flocked into the path of totality for the 2017 total solar eclipse across the United States. The same will happen on a larger scale for the forthcoming 2024 eclipse. Imagine being caught off guard by guests wanting to book a tour or room in a few years for an eclipse or other astronomical phenomena.

In writing my own book about astrotourism, *Dark Skies: A Practical Guide to Astrotourism*, I was struck by the as-yet-untapped opportunity for growth in the astrotourism sector. Many of the experiences and locations I shared in that book are increasingly known by those of us who love to travel to see the wonders of the night sky, but there are still a far greater majority of those who have never heard of them or experienced what they have to offer.

When you have completed reading *Astrotourism: Star Gazers, Eclipse Chasers and the Astronomical Rise of the Dark Sky Movement,* you'll have a greater awareness and appreciation of the astrotourism industry, if you're not inspired to apply it directly. You will have the opportunity to tap into your own passion for the subject and apply it to your career; whether you were inspired by an astronomical experience as a child like I was or find yourself motivated by the economics, astrotourism is on the rise, here to stay, and you'll be better prepared to take advantage of while simultaneously protecting one of our great natural resources.

Acknowledgments

I want to acknowledge a dark sky and how its lullaby serenades our hearts, minds, bodies and souls.

Introduction

The foundations of civilization are grounded in the night sky, as the stars have been stitched into the human race's history. There was no place on the planet where people did not commune with the darkness of night and watch the cavalcade of stars sweep over the Earth in an endless procession. Today, we are witnessing the disappearing view of the night sky in the course of one human lifetime, after it had been here with us for hundreds of thousands of human lifetimes.

Here is a nursery rhyme that you may know but four lines of. People are mostly oblivious to something they do not know exists while knowing it exists. We know intellectually that stars are in the sky, while at the same time, not seeing and experiencing the stars in the sky. It is a cognitive dissonance that is under the surface. Most people are born and live under a dome of light, yet we learn this as one of our very first songs.

> Twinkle, twinkle, little star,
> How I wonder what you are!
> Up above the world so high,
> Like a diamond in the sky.
> Twinkle, Twinkle, little star
> How I wonder what you are?

We thought that was all there was to it. The rest of the poem was forgotten because it had lost its meaning to modern civilizations. We have literally become adrift from our ties to the cosmos because it has ceased to be a part of our daily lives. We have forgotten what an indispensable part the stars were to our very existence. The rest of the poem illustrates.

> When the blazing sun is gone,
> When he nothing shines upon,
> Then you show your little light,
> Twinkle, twinkle, all the night.
> Then the trav'ller in the dark,

Thanks you for your tiny spark,
He could not see which way to go,
If you did not twinkle so.
In the dark blue sky you keep,
And often thro' my curtains peep,
For you never shut your eye,
Till the sun is in the sky.
'Tis your bright and tiny spark,
Lights the trav'ller in the dark,
Tho' I know not what you are,
Twinkle, twinkle, little star.

"Twinkle" was published in 1806 when a person needed the stars for their survival. Those tiny sparks that we relied on to get home for hundreds of thousands of years are now all but invisible to nearly one billion people. Though we do not see them, we can still hear their call.

Anthropogenic light pollution is the main driver of astrotourism. If light pollution did not exist to the extent that it does, astrotourism would hardly get a mention save for the occasional meteor showers, rare eclipses, and journeys to the far north by the intrepid traveler to see the auroral displays. Our relationship with the night sky has been stripped from our daily lives and along with it the mystery, romance, fear, magic, spirituality, joy, and peace that goes with communing with the stars.

Life is born in darkness. When people have near-death experiences, they speak of "going to the light." It is highly ironic that we fear the former but crave the latter to such a degree that we have set the night on fire with our lights without understanding the consequences like the plastics that have been released into our environment over the last 70 years and are found at the bottom of the ocean floor and the top of our tallest mountains. Like light pollution, we did not see it coming.

People want to escape the light-polluted confines of a big city and get under the stars and experience the night, and by creating a monetary value on a pristine night sky, people will be compelled to protect it—it is not our nature to be driven by the higher angels of ourselves but by our purses. This is not necessarily the case for generations X, Y, and Z. Like the Baby Boomers once were, they are full of ideas and desire to create a better world, not just get ahead in it; for them, it has become a matter of planetary survival. Astrotourism is a step toward that, and in its own way, can transform the consumer to have a greater understanding of the world they live in and their impact upon it.

Hopefully, by the time a first-time astrotourist returns home, they will see artificial light at night (ALAN) in a new way and take steps locally to reignite the stars in the sky by raising awareness of the issue of protecting the night. The astrotourism market will have a direct impact that will amplify the protection of a nocturnal landscape full of wildlife that relies on their connection, as we once did, on the ability to see the stars.

CHAPTER 1

Defining Astrotourism

Keep your eyes on the stars and your feet on the ground.
—Theodore Roosevelt (26th President
of the USA 1858–1919)

Astrotourism is such a new phenomenon the word has yet to be found in the *Merriam-Webster Dictionary.* It was once called "astronomy tourism" and composed primarily of professional and amateur astronomers. In the last three decades, a dark sky has become a rare commodity, and people are traveling to experience a pristine night sky and all that it has to offer, one that is void of light pollution.

It is an emerging type of tourism, and the definition remains fluid. It can be described as a segment of the tourist market in which travelers journey to experience celestial and space occurrences; however, another definition may include anything that is space-themed, for example, viewing a rocket launch or a satellite or rocket re-entering the Earth's atmosphere staying in a space-décor hotel, or visiting a planetarium.

This newly formed segment of the travel market may also include visiting archeological sites, where megaliths were built to measure the movements of celestial bodies; traveling to locations where cultures celebrate specific celestial events; viewing atmospheric anomalies, like sun dogs, zodiacal glow, green flash, rainbows, or moon halos. Also included, the measuring devices created by scientists that calculated celestial movements such as astronomical clocks, sundials, astronomical mechanisms, and works created by artists that depicted the sun, moon, stars, and other sky-born events. The leisure travel market off-planet Earth and into space is budding, bringing "high altitude" and "outer space" travel under the tent of astrotourism as a subset.

Astrotourism is now a thing.
—Condé Nast Magazine February 27, 2017

This textbook is for those who would serve this new segment of the travel market, such as tour operators, hotel or resort managers, an outfitter, a tour guide, or anyone in the hospitality industry who seeks to attract and accommodate the astrotourist. This new travel trend is attracting a new kind of tourist who is choosing a destination in order to enjoy the beauty of the universe they live in but one that they rarely see; when visiting "black sky" locations, astrotourists are distributing their money and ecological footprint more evenly across the planet.

With the rise of astrotourism, local governments pass laws and enforce ordinances to eliminate or dramatically curb light pollution like "Bill S.1937," which is currently moving its way through the Massachusetts Senate. This oversight will protect our dark skies, a rapidly disappearing resource, and support and foster an economic engine that brings substantive revenues from travelers into otherwise overlooked regions.

> *Astrotourism, the latest trend in travel, sees travelers search for "black sky" locations on the ultimate stargazing holidays.*
> —Absolutely London

> *Astrotourism is the latest travel trend on the rise and one that Airbnb is championing. The company has seen significant year-on-year growth in places like: La Palma, Spain (90%), Antofagasta, Chile (327%), Kiruna, Sweden (134%), and Yarmouth, Canada (221%).*
> —Associated Press, July 11, 2018

If you are a typical North American or European, you have never seen the Milky Way or a night sky in its pristine state. How rare is it to see a Dark Sky? It is a jaw-dropping statistic that 80 percent of all the land on Earth and 99 percent of North America and Europe's population lives under so much light pollution to make the Milky Way virtually invisible.[1]

Scarcity drives up value, both intrinsic and economical. As of 2017, the World Population Review determined that about 1,109,599,402 people live in North America and Europe; of these, only 11,095, 994 have a view of a truly dark night sky and the myriad of stars there. Those who live in these dark sky areas are under the false assumption that everyone else sees this and are well-positioned to open the uninitiated eyes to reveal a night previously unknown to them.

How many stars are there to see? The first edition of the *Bright Star Catalogue,* published in 1930 by an American astronomer, Frank Schlesinger, identified the number of stars that could be viewed with the naked eye; this number was updated in subsequent editions. Due to multiple viewing factors (the presence of haze on the horizon, proximity of light pollution, humidity, the observer's altitude, quality of one's eyesight, etc.), there is some disagreement among scientists about the number of visible stars. According to the astronomer Dorrit Hoffleit, who wrote the last edition of *Bright Star Catalog* in 1964, humans can see about 9,095 stars with the naked eye. This includes all of the stars in both the Northern and Southern Hemispheres. As we can only be standing in one hemisphere, only half that number can be seen at any given time. With a pair of 50 mm binoculars, 100,000 stars are visible, and with a small, three-inch telescope, visibility explodes to 5,000,000!

Astrotourism is more than stargazing, as it includes traveling to see other celestial phenomena. The northern lights, or aurora borealis, is an attraction so spectacular and relatively predictable that multiple tour groups across the world have been in business for decades bringing people to see this cosmic event. According to *Science Nordic,*

> Tromsø Norway has an increase in the number of aurora borealis tourists—partly because major international newspapers have featured articles about the aurora in northern Norway, and partly because of the amazing photos and videos that have gone viral on social media.

The speed that photos are being seen by people worldwide is astonishing compared to just 20 years ago. Once the domain of professional photographers who had to go through the time-consuming process of developing film before sending photos to a media outlet, which in turn had to print and distribute the content, can now be dispersed almost instantly by anybody with a mobile device and a social media account. Technology catapulted astrotourism like nothing else ever has.

Astrotourism includes eclipse chasers who will go to great lengths and distances to see an event that is only minutes in length, a reflection of how passionate astrotourists can be. It is estimated that 88 percent of American adults—about 215 million people—watched the 2017 solar eclipse, either in person or electronically.[2] It is over 50 million more than those who voted in the 2020 presidential election counting both sides. The astrotourist could be anybody who travels away from the city to experience the magic of a full moon.

> *The Moon is the first milestone on the road to the stars.*
>   —Arthur C. Clarke

Only in today's world of electric nights are we unaware of the potency of a moonlit night and how much illumination is cast upon the ground. All of us see the moon, even at the bottom of a high-rise skyscraper canyon that is our major metropolitan area, but we do not experience a moonlit evening and all of its ghostly appeal. To see the landscape in such clarity in only shades of gray, silver, and black stirs something primal in us. There is little or no need for artificial illumination to navigate the nocturnal landscape under a moon gorged with the sun's reflective light. The moon's shadow's intensity will never be realized unless one travels to a place where the moon is the brightest object in the night sky.

A dark sky and all the stars it holds were once in everybody's suburban backyard, but it has all but disappeared in the last 75 years. Because of light pollution, people have to journey, sometimes great distances and spend considerable money to see a starry sky. Starlight has taken millions of light-years to reach our eyes, and it is being "drowned out" at the finish line by streetlights and the sea of artificial light at night (ALAN). This veil of light has been pulled over our eyes, and the greatest portion of the world's population can no longer experience the dark of night. The irony here is that anthropogenic light pollution has both spurred and catapulted the astrotourism industry while at the same time remains its greatest threat.

Scores of articles on astrotourism and light pollution show up in *National Geographic, The Guardian, USA Today, The New York Times, The Washington Post,* and even a Jeopardy game show. "Astronomy buffs visit Idaho for the USA's first dark sky reserve; oddly, part of it is this resort area with a bright name." The answer in the form of a question, "What is Sun Valley?" The Central Idaho Dark Sky Reserve gained this classification in

2017 from the International Dark-Sky Association (IDA); more on the IDA and its influence on astrotourism in Chapter 5.

Astrotourism and space tourism have sometimes been used interchangeably; however, a distinction separates the two. In the former, the tourist remains on the ground looking up; the latter takes the tourist up to look down. Chapter 6 is dedicated to the work in the field of tourist space flight that will "Boldly take tourists where no tourist has gone before." The fact that you may know the reference (*Star Trek*) is proof that there is a craving for the cosmos in all of us, and it has been woven into the fabric of our cultures across the globe throughout time. Today, astrotourists are literally on a "star trek."

CHAPTER 2

Our Link to the Stars

Of all things visible, the highest is the heaven of the fixed stars.
—Nicolaus Copernicus (astronomer)

Though astronomers, both professional and amateur, were the original astrotourists, many people seeking dark skies are neither. As humans, we are linked to the sky above and have been as long as we have had the awareness that our closest star makes a daily appearance in the east, rising like magic, emerging from the horizon. Early humans might have thought it was coming right out of the Earth, as it does appear to do so. As the sun ascends skyward, our shadows grow shorter with each passing hour until it reaches the zenith, when our shadow disappears and is born anew as the sun begins its journey back into the bed of the Earth's edge.

The end of the day was determined once the sun went out of sight, but it changed color, echoing its appearance at dawn before it did. The rich saturated colors accompanied the appearance and disappearance of the clouds we attribute with a sun's rise and set. For most people who leave a central metropolitan area to travel to an astrotourist destination, the sunrise and sunset can be some of the most memorable moments of their trips. This brings us to the phenomenon known as the golden hour and the blue hour, both of which are significant because of the photographic opportunities they provide.

The golden hour is the period of time the color of the sky goes from red and orange to yellow or, as its name suggests, golden tones, having a warm color temperature. Lighting is soft, diffused, and with little contrast since the sun is low in the sky. The sky has a deep blue hue with a cold color temperature and saturated colors during the blue hour. At the beginning (evening) and the end (morning), a gradient of colors, from blue to orange, can be seen right in the place of sunset and sunrise.[1]

It could be said that the most prominent and daily dose of star watching occurs when we are tracking our sun. The vacation-of-choice for Baby Boomers was often going to sunny places or escaping the cold to chase our closest star for its warmth. The World Youth Student and Educational (WYSE) Travel Confederation recently surveyed more than 34,000 people from 137 countries and found that young travelers are not interested in the traditional sun, sea, and sand holidays as were previous generations.[2] They are more intrepid seekers, longing for the unusual, scarce, and strange. A night ablaze with stars is one of the true exotic views in the world today. Some destinations are specifically designed to cater to the astrotourist, and more are being designated each day.

> *Across the planet, travelers are now seeking out the world's last-remaining dark skies where they can get a clear, unpolluted view of the stars.*
>
> —*The Lonely Planet* June 12, 2019

The ancients tracked our nearest star with such dedication that even scientists in modern times are left astounded by their accuracy, using nothing that resembled the sophisticated tools we have today. The oldest known calendar is dated to 8000 BCE. The original calendars were lunar in nature and based on the moon phases, not the sun's movement.

Though the Gregorian calendar is used by most countries globally, a large segment of the population still adheres to the lunar calendar to indicate their holidays and New Year. Even some Western holidays are based on celestial events. In 325 CE, the Council of Nicaea established that Easter would be held on the first Sunday after the first full moon occurring on or after the vernal equinox. One of the most important holidays celebrated in Christianity compels the celebrant to track not one but two astronomical events.

Though billions of people of all faiths do not necessarily travel to see a full moon, they are watching the sky and the movement of our closest celestial body to determine when it is time to celebrate. The ancients had to track the sun, moon, and stars to know when to plant and harvest. They knew that a week before and after the full moon was the best time to travel and waited until then to take their trips to markets because it is then bright enough to travel at night.

Human's connection to the night sky and all of its stars is inescapable, and millions are traveling to recapture the enchantment, awe, and reverence that stargazing brings. The stars overhead connect us with the rest of what is out there and with eternity itself, as starlight began its journey years ago and traveled trillions of miles to reach us. It takes the sun's light eight minutes to reach the Earth, so we see the sun as it was eight minutes earlier. We are looking back in time, and we can do that any night we can see the stars. By the time starlight reaches our eyes, the star from which it came may have burnt out thousands of years ago, but we do not know it yet.

Astrotourist have a sense of belonging to the universe and not just to the world. They seek the quiet and solitude that comes from being in a pristine location. They return to their lives with a renewed vitality, as if the weight of everyday life were lifted from their shoulders, if only for a night or two. One of the most famous paintings in the world is *Starry Night* by Vincent Van Gogh.

Figure 2.1 Van Gogh's Starry Night 1889 Museum of Modern Art NYC

A night sky full of stars is more moving than the greatest painting or humanmade monument could ever be and has inspired great minds from all walks of life to try to capture it in words:

For my part, I know nothing with any certainty, but the sight of the stars makes me dream.

—Vincent van Gogh—Artist

Stars are good, too. I wish I could get some to put in my hair. Nevertheless, I suppose I never can. You would be surprised to find how far off they are, for they do not look it.

—Mark Twain—Author

It is not in the stars to hold our destiny but in ourselves.

—William Shakespeare—Playwright

Though my soul may set in darkness, it will rise in perfect light; I have loved the stars too truly to be fearful of the night.

—Sarah Williams—Poet

Only in the darkness can you see the light.

—Reverend Martin Luther King Jr.—Civil Rights Activist

The nitrogen in our DNA, the calcium in our teeth, the iron in our blood, the carbon in our apple pies were made in the interiors of collapsing stars. We are made of star-stuff.

—Carl Sagan—Astronomer

What is so amazing that keeps us stargazing, and what do we think we might see?

—Kermit the Frog—Amphibian

The oldest stories ever told are those about the stars, and those stories have been forgotten by most of humanity, yet humans still look up and have a need to "connect the dots."

The idioms "connect the dots" and "join-the-dots" are twentieth-century phrases taken from a type of puzzle invented sometime around that century. In a "connect-the-dots" puzzle or "join-the-dots" puzzle, various numbered dots are arranged across the page in a seemingly random fashion. However, when the participant connects the dots, a drawing appears.[2]

My assertion is that the original "connect the dots" was not from a 20th-century puzzle but from making sense of the dots in a night sky thousands of years ago, creating the constellations we know today. The astrotourist wants to hear the stories of old, retold. They have a genuine curiosity to understand the night sky and be exposed to the knowledge and wisdom passed down for thousands of years.

Ancient forbearers knew the night sky like the back of their hand. The constellations oriented them in a literal sense—as vital navigation tools—but in a spiritual one as well, serving as vivid reminders of their mythologies and place in the universe. Still, today, knowing the constellations can be a source of both satisfying knowledge and humbling awe.[3]

When travelers learn about the night sky at a dark sky destination, they learn something that can be taken back home and shared with others. The astrotourist will return from their trip not only with photos or souvenirs but with knowledge and the ability to guide another person around the night sky. I have yet to meet anyone who did not desire to identify a constellation beyond the asterisms they know, the Big Dipper and Orion's Belt.

Astrotourists are adventure travelers who seek far-flung places to get away from it all so that they can connect with it all. The night sky is not static but a dynamic skyscape revealing a new star, a new constellation, and a new perspective with every hour that passes. Those who travel to see the Zion National Park in Utah or Yosemite in California or Mt. Fuji in Japan, or Kilimanjaro in Tanzania will see natural monuments that will not move anytime soon. To lie flat on one's back, looking upon a clear night, and watch the sky roll from east to west, is to witness the planet itself turning in its relationship with the vast reaches of space.

The night holds an endless and ancient enthrallment that has lasted hundreds of thousands of years, and the growing trend of astrotourism is reigniting that fascination by reconnecting people with the darkness of an unfettered night sky.

CHAPTER 3

Star Seeker Trends

Dwell on the beauty of life. Watch the stars, and see yourself running with them.

—Marcus Aurelius (Roman Emperor)

Since 1979, when J.L. Crompton published his paper, "Motivations for Pleasure Vacations," there have been numerous studies on what drives tourists to any given place. With other follow-up studies, the industry adopted some tenants regarding push and pull factors related to tourism in general. The push drives someone from where they live to go someplace else, and the pull lures and shows them the magnetism of a destination.

A push would be the desire for escape, relaxation, adventure, social interaction, health, or prestige; the pull is the appeal and lure of a destination, for example, the recreational facilities, entertainment, culture, cuisine, or sunshine that is available. Astrotourist motivations closely align with the precepts laid out in Graham M.S. Dann's, "Agony, ego-enhancement and tourism" study, particularly those stemming from "anomie" and "ego-enhancement" in the tourist himself.

However, to the best of one's knowledge, anomie has not been associated with tourism. It is claimed that a possible push factor for travel lies in the desire to transcend the feeling of isolation obtained in everyday life, where the tourist simply wishes to get away from it all.[1] Within the span of a human lifetime, civilization lost something that bound us all together for hundreds of thousands of years, that created a sense of belonging to something greater than self: Our love for the stars and the feeling that comes with standing under the dome of a night sky.

Light pollution is a societal issue, as ALAN, (Artificial Light At Night) is ubiquitous; its impact across national borders and continents is cross-generational and not species-specific. The effects of this new nightscape have not been fully realized nor adequately studied. The planet and those living on it will benefit from curbing light pollution's spread, as it has disrupted the rhythm of day and night that has been established over millions of years. In addition to the ecological benefits, dark sky initiatives and practices provide a revenue stream for hard-pressed places to attract tourists.

Oxford, New Zealand, was working to cement its future as a tourist destination for stargazers.

> We wanted to get Oxford on the map as a destination, and having the observatory is a unique attraction that gives visitors a reason to stay overnight and come and see the night sky. It is all about getting visitors into Oxford, and that then supports other local businesses, like accommodations and restaurants, too,

says James Moffat, a volunteer who has been working to create the "Inland Scenic Star Trail."[2]

The collateral benefits of dark skies, and the initiatives to keep them pristine to attract tourists, are often overlooked, if not below the horizons of people's understanding in the first place. This book is about more than sightseeing or traveling to remote and untouched places on the planet to witness the stars and other celestial events, as there is a causal relationship between light pollution and astrotourism. There is no place on the planet that we, as humans, have not yet touched. Our anthropogenic footprint is found from Antarctica to the top of Mauna Kea in Hawaii and Mt. Everest in the Himalayas to the bottom of the deepest part of our oceans.

As the world's population increases, so will light usage, and with light usage comes the creation of greenhouse gases and light pollution that create sky glow. Skyglow is anathema to astrotourism and can have a detrimental impact on a stargazing site from as far away as 400 kilometers.

The beneficiaries of dark sky initiatives go beyond the tourist trade. Humans can quantify this value using a pecuniary meter stick, but wildlife has no way to measure the value of life, as night pollinators, bats, fireflies, migratory birds, turtles, and other wildlife depend on their view of the stars and moon to navigate toward safety, food sources, and potential mates. As we humans embrace the dark and take the necessary steps to protect it, we become stewards for the many creatures with whom we share the planet and the night.

Here are some other drivers for the rise in astrotourism: as of 2017, there were over 7,000 commercial aircraft (in the United States alone) that carried approximately 1.32 billion international tourists worldwide, with the largest number (670.6 million) traveling to Europe and the Asia-Pacific region (323.1 million).[3] With this increase in traffic, certain tourist destinations are being trodden to death, becoming ruins before their time. Swarming like locusts in a feeding frenzy, popular historical, cultural, and natural sites worldwide are in danger.

Governments are starting to charge for places that were once free and limit visitors' number to protect the integrity and beauty of attractions. Parc Guell, one of Barcelona's largest green spaces, limits visitors to 800 a day and charges a gate fee. Though the controversy persists about whether or not it is appropriate to charge, the fact remains that people create an impact when they travel, and too many people can destroy the very thing they have traveled to visit. A confluence of macroeconomic factors and changing business trends have led more tourists crowding to popular destinations. That has led to environmental degradation, dangerous conditions, and the immiseration and pricing-out of locals in many places. Massive crowds are causing environmental degradation, dangerous conditions, and the immiseration of pricing out locals, as international tourist arrivals around the world have gone from a little less than 70 million as of 1960 to 1.4 billion today: Mass tourism, again, is a very new thing, and a huge thing.[4]

To ameliorate this concentration, astrotourism spreads out both the number of tourists and its economic impact to the benefit of rural and more remote destinations. Astrotourism is an environmentally friendly, authentic, and sustainable way to travel to empower lesser-known rural communities economically.[5] It will advance mom-and-pop businesses in underdeveloped locales that, up until the recent ALAN explosion, may have thought they had little to offer in the way of an attraction. As there is no major capital necessary to create a Dark Sky attraction, it is a low-cost, low-impact tourism form.

Through Airbnb, local experts, who do not provide rental or accommodations, now offer over 30,000 unique experiences, activities, and tours. This service began in 2016 and grew 25 times faster than rental homes did in its first year. People want a memory to take home, and travelers are more likely to remember a singular experience than what kind of room they stayed in or house they rented, novelty dwellings not-withstanding.

Experiences can expand one's awareness, and learning something new can be stimulating for all ages. As we expand our knowledge, our sense of self expands along with it. Learning to navigate the night sky and discovering its cultural relevance is something the astrotourist can share with others. Getting to know your way around the night sky is not something that takes years to understand, but it is something that will remain with you for a lifetime.

Part of Dann's postulation for the desire to travel is the need to have one's ego enhanced or boosted from time to time. In sociological parlance, the desire for such recognition by others is often described in terms of status; on their return, a further boost can be given to one's ego in the recounting of holiday experiences—trip dropping.[1] It is inherently cool to travel to see the aurora borealis or an exotic location that has not been contaminated by the trappings of modern living, where the stars are laid out like a banquet for our eyes to feast upon.

People and communities wanting to develop an astrotourism revenue stream are incentivized to protect their natural surroundings by curbing outdoor lighting. This, in turn, saves energy, reduces carbon footprint, and supports the ecosystem by not disrupting the nocturnal landscape.

How is the value of a dark sky calculated? Terrell Galaway, a Ph.D. in economics, writes, "If a family pays $5000 to travel to a place to see a pristine night sky, then it is already worth that much."

> Astrotourism offers a sort of "draw-down space" and funnels the cosmos [into a] peephole to be "consumed" by the tourist gaze (at a price). Barriers to entry can be fairly high (as befits the niche concept), with the result that it is not so easy for competitors to jump on the bandwagon. Location is critical, and although the night skies can be observed with the naked eye, the whole point of the astronomical quest is to see ever deeper into space. To this end, the better one's equipment, the pricier and the less portable it is likely to be. Making the most of "nothing": astrotourism, the Sublime, and the Karoo as a "space destination."[6]

Citing a newsroom report from Airbnb in 2018, "The United States, France, and Italy are the three countries with the highest number of stargazing-ready listings on Airbnb."

As in the Colorado Plateau, the effect of dark skies on the state economies is quite large. Over the next 10 years, visitors will spend nearly $2.5 billion visiting National Park Service (NPS) parks in the Dark Sky Cooperative trying to see a dark sky at night. This additional $2.45 billion in spending creates $1.68 billion in additional value-added for the local state economies. The total effect of all of this additional spending is to create an additional 52,257 jobs that increase wages in the states by over $1,094 million.[7]

A small but growing number of park visitors seek astrotourism opportunities. In some areas, such as the southwestern United States, this is more than an idea; it is a current economic driver.[8] The dark skies of the Colorado Plateau can be used and promoted as a magnet for tourism.

Crucially, from an economic standpoint, the single most important thing about dark-sky tourism is that it necessitates one or more overnight stays. The NPS estimates that the average spending per party per day is about $90 for non-local day trips. For parties staying overnight at an NPS lodge, this spending rises to over $390. For those staying in motels outside the park, the amount is a little over $270. In other words, inducing visitors to stay overnight can increase spending several-fold.[9]

Astrotourism benefits a municipality, as would any destination that attracts people from out-of-state and beyond, but beyond the purely monetary allowances, this form of tourism demands preserving a resource that has a collateral value that goes beyond the economic metric; it contributes to the community as a whole.

CHAPTER 4

The Present and Future Astrotourist

I will love the light for it will show me the way and yet I will endure the darkness, for it shows me the stars.

—Og Mandino (author)

Astrotourists are explorers at their core, whether they travel to some remote location to see a distant object in space or stay in their backyards and explore the night sky that revolves overhead. These are people who keep looking and learning, allied with sustainability travelers, eco-travelers, adventure travelers, outdoor enthusiasts, hunters, fishers, campers, backpackers, river rafters, sailors, trekkers, and any other travelers who find themselves under a dark sky anywhere in the world. Some go to great extremes. A hardy lot, they endure winter's breath, stay up all hours of the night and lose sleep to see the stars. However, this is not to imply that astrotourism experiences need be uncomfortable. Chilling out on a comfy blanket under a clear warm summer night sky is an easy sell.

Because of population densities and the recent phenomenon of light pollution, these tourists are primarily from urban and metropolitan areas, as this is where the overwhelming percentage of ALAN can be found. If you are a typical North American or European, you have never seen the Milky Way or a night sky in its pristine state. How rare is it to see a dark sky? More than 80 percent of the world and more than 99 percent of the U.S. and European populations live under light-polluted skies. The Milky Way is hidden from more than one-third of humanity, including 60 percent of Europeans and 80 percent of North Americans.[1]

Astrotourists have environmental underpinnings in their value set, as dark skies are a natural resource that needs protection. Consider these tourists preservationists and ecologists, as they understand the need for

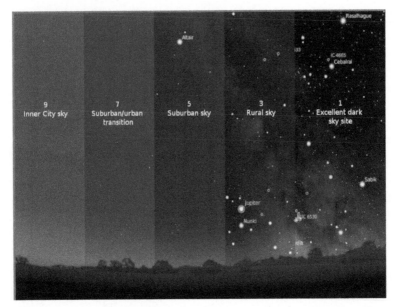

Figure 4.1 The Bortle scale

Source: John C. Barentine

earth stewardship. Astrotourists participate in astronomy and the associated culture, making them curious people who are eager to learn. They enjoy sharing what they know and connecting with others who have the same passion.

Over half (56 percent) of global travelers agree that traveling has taught them invaluable life skills, and in 2019, we saw a rise in people's desire to learn something new while away from home as well as an increase in volunteering and skills-based vacations across generations.[3] The astrotourist spans a considerable range of income demographics, as some seek nothing more than an open field with an unobstructed view of the night, one that is void of illuminated impediments; others prefer ultra-luxury accommodations, hoping to see rare celestial events.

Some come with nothing more than their unaided eyes, while others sport optical equipment that can range from twenty dollars to thousands of dollars. Astrotourists can include the highly privileged who have the disposable income to purchase lavish package expeditions that may involve the charter of a yacht, luxury liner, or even private aircraft to chase an eclipse.

There is a much larger segment of astrotourists who are sustainable travelers, as the very thing they are traveling to see requires a conscious effort to preserve it. These travelers venture into the great unknown or visit a national, state, or county park, the great known. As sustainable travel is increasing worldwide, those who seek to cater to the astrotourist will enjoy the upswing in that segment of the travel market, as it includes all things under a dark sky.

- 72 percent of travelers believe that people need to act now and make sustainable travel choices to save the planet for future generations.
- 73 percent of global travelers intend to stay at least once in an eco-friendly or green accommodation when looking at the year ahead.
- 70 percent of global travelers say they would be more likely to book an accommodation knowing it was eco-friendly,
- This is the fourth consecutive year that Booking.com research has seen this figure trend up, from 62 percent in 2016 to 65 percent in 2017 and 68 percent in 2018.
- 55 percent of global travelers report being more determined to make sustainable travel choices than they were a year ago, but barriers include a lack of knowledge and available or appealing options when trying to put this into practice. These sustainable decisions include accommodation.[2]

It is possible to drive to many astrotourist destinations. However, airline travel will be a preferable mode of transportation to escape the sky glow created by light pollution in the heavily populated portions of the Northeast of the United States, the population centers of Europe, and other locations. Using satellite imaging, it is possible to identify the places where ALAN is most pronounced, and my assertion is that these locations would be a likely place to focus marketing efforts to generate clients.

Markets change to meet tourists' desire to respond to the planetary impact created by fossil fuel burning. Airlines are a major contributor to a traveler's carbon footprint and the detriment it causes to the environment, and sustainable travelers are conscious of this fact. Carbon dioxide,

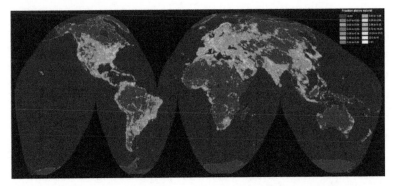

Figure 4.2 Night atlas Falchi et al., Science Advances 10 June 2016:Vol. 2, no. 6, e1600377 (DOI: 10.1126/sciadv.1600377)

a major greenhouse gas, will reach over 900 million metric tons in 2018 and triple by 2050.[3] Further evidence supporting the growth in sustainable travel trends is that airlines and other groups offer carbon offsets to allow a traveler to contribute to carbon sinks, tree planting, solar, and wind power projects. More people purchase these carbon credits every year to offset fuel consumption and greenhouse gas emissions that come with air travel.

The vacation for the baby boomers was often going to sunny places or escaping the cold to chase the sun, but to quote Bob Dylan, himself a boomer, "The times they are a-changin." The World Youth Student and Educational (WYSE) Travel Confederation, which recently surveyed more than 34,000 people from 137 countries, found that young travelers are not interested in "the traditional sun, sea, and sand holidays" as previous generations were. As stated by Patrick Quayle, vice president for international planning at United Airlines, "We are millennials, and we are looking to have different travel experiences than our parents."[4]

Astrotourists are resolute travelers longing for the unusual, scarce, and strange. A night ablaze with stars is one of the true exotic views in the world today, and people have to travel further afield to find a pristine night sky. Most people experience seeing a dark sky for the first time when they are on a camping trip. Together, the Coleman Company, Inc. and The Outdoor Foundation created the 2017 American Camper Report and found that:

- About 40 million people camp every year:
- 52 percent staying 1–2 nights
- 35 percent staying 3–4 nights
- 7 percent staying 5–6 nights
- 5 percent staying 7 or more nights

Of those who responded:

- 72 percent stayed within 150 miles of home
- 5 percent would drive 301–500 miles to their final destination
- 11 percent of all camping participants in 2016 were new to camping, about 4.7 million people
- 26 percent were young adults between the ages of 25 and 34
- 92 percent of first-time campers reported that they were "very likely" or "likely" to go camping again next year.

Therein lies the power of the call of the wild and its connection to astrotourism. The survey asked people to rank their top ten night time activities, and there are the top three:

- (81 percent) was sitting around a campfire, what might be referred to as "stone age TV."
- (63 percent) was star gazing or "stone age IMAX."
- (52 percent) was grilling or "stone-age cooking."

Homo sapiens have evolved; our tastes have not changed so much as we still enjoy sitting around a fire, the stars, and cooking over the flames.

To illustrate the causal relationship of the rise of industrialization and urbanization to astrotourism, the following is offered to provide historical context. At the age of nine, Thomas Hiram Holding[5] (1844–1930) went on a camping trip with his family along the Mississippi River and then participated in a wagon train across America's great plains, still able to see the great buffalo herds.

He returned to England and began work as a tailor. London's extensive metropolis was choked with soot and smog from the coal burned to drive engines and produce heat. To escape the maddening crowds, he and friends would take trips along a river or bicycle paths, bringing along their gear so they could overnight. No doubt, the breath of fresh air was a tonic to the body, mind, and soul. In 1897, at the age of 52, he built a tent (using his tailoring skills) to pack onto a bicycle, took a trip, and wrote a book about the experience, cementing his place in tourism history.

He became the foremost expert in recreational camping, and his book, *The Camper's Handbook*, published in 1908, is still available today.[6] It is not hard to imagine what the night skies in London would have looked like at the turn of the 19th century. In the same way that our camping forebears sought wild places to escape the city to get a breath of fresh air and commune with nature, we in the 21st century are seeking the same escape; yet for today's urban dweller, it is the chance to flee the city lights so that we can commune with the cosmos.

Because camping is likely the first time many people see the stars in a pristine night sky, and because 92 percent of first-time campers report they would do it again, it is easy to extrapolate that the wonder and awe induced by a night sky creates a compelling argument that the stars had something to do with it.

In 2020, *The Dyrt*, a top-ranked campground search app, has seen their user traffic climb 400 percent from this same time last year (July 2019). Paid memberships on the camping app, which boasts more than 15 million users, have increased by 500 percent in the last two weeks alone (from July 1 to July 14, 2020), a trend that coincides with the most significant increase of Google "camping" searches in nearly a decade.[7] Who are the future astrotourists? Given that well over 800 million people who live in Europe and North America can no longer see the Milky Way, if only one-half of 1 percent take the spirited step to escape the cacophony of urban light pollution, to step into the wild as Thomas Hiram Holding did, there is a potential audience of approximately 4 million people looking for a dark sky and a night full of stars.

The majority of campers (92 percent) actually bring some type of technology with them while camping.[8] Today 81 percent of Americans own a smartphone, up from just 35 percent since 2011.[9]

It is apparent that with the proliferation of smartphones and the numerous applications available designed to navigate the stars, more people will be better equipped to take on exploring the mysterious nocturnal skyscape.

Two generations ago, this technology could hardly be imagined except in the realm of science fiction. The computing power of mobile devices puts a wealth of information into the user's hands to make their time under the night sky more enjoyable and educational. They have been given the tools to connect the constellations' dots, track satellites, and receive coronal mass ejection (CME) notices and other data—astrotourists are techies.

As of 2009, Carl Sagan's *Cosmos* series (first aired September 28, 1980) was still the most widely watched PBS series globally. It was broadcast in more than 60 countries and seen by over 500 million people. Since its broadcast, the show was considered highly significant; David Itzkoff of *The New York Times* described it as "a watershed moment for science-themed television programming." The enthusiasm for space and the science behind our exploration of it continues to this day in ever-increasing numbers.

In 2014, *Cosmos: A Spacetime Odyssey*, hosted by Neil Degrasse-Tyson, received an unprecedented rollout in 180 countries with a whopping 135 million people, including 45 million in the U.S., watching at least some of the 13-part science series. Overall, it aired on all 90 National Geographic Channels, as well as 120 Fox-branded channels in 125 countries, making this the largest global launch ever for a television series.

Rick Kissell, *Variety Magazine* (July 7, 2014)

Astrotourists, like science fiction fans, are curious about what goes on in outer space. This may provide some clues into how to market to this segment of the populace. Science fiction is global in its appeal, and the *Star Wars* and *Star Trek* franchises have generated billions of dollars from their avid fans for over half a century. *Star Trek* was released in 1966, and the first *Star Wars* movie was released in 1977, the same year the Voyager 1 and 2 space probes were launched. Voyager is continuing its journey, now 13 billion miles away, and science fiction movies continue to play at theaters near you or on streaming services.

These movies beckoned the viewer to travel to the stars and experience the great, vast expanse of space. The revenues from *Close Encounters of the Third Kind; Contact; Guardians of the Galaxy; 2001: A Space Odyssey; Aliens 1, 2, 3, 4; The Martian; Gravity; Apollo 13; The Fifth Element; Marooned; Avatar; Ad Astra; Interstellar;* and so on is in the hundreds of billions of dollars. If you total up all of the *Star Wars* movie receipts from 1995, this franchise by itself has sold nearly 300,000 million tickets in the United States alone.[10]

Disney World spent $1 billion on their new *Star Wars: Galaxy's Edge* attraction.[11] This audience loves star travel from this massive pool of people, even if it is only make-believe. To postulate that even if only one-half of 1 percent of the *Star Wars* ticket buyers come over to the "dark side" to see the stars, it still represents 1,500,000 people. These are merely speculations of the number of people who may be inclined to take a trip away from the city lights see a dark sky, but it has already been demonstrated that this audience will travel to and purchase a vicarious ticket experience of traveling to the stars. These tourists need not journey to a galaxy far, far away but be provided the place where a dark sky still exists, albeit if they have to drive or fly to it. A more likely group of people to trend toward astrotourism would be those who visit planetaria.

Zeiss Optical Company demonstrated the first projection planetarium at the Deutsches Museum in Munich, Germany, in 1923. By 1970—the Apollo moon program's height—there were an estimated 700 to 800 planetariums globally, half of them less than six years old; 25 years later, that number has more than doubled to a little over 2,000.[12]

The author's first experience of a virtual night inside a domed enclosure was at the Hayden Planetarium in New York City at age eight and was never forgotten (nor was the exit music, *Fanfare for the Common Man,* by Aaron Copeland). The importance of a music track will be discussed further in Chapter 13. For city dwellers, this is a taste of what a starry night sky would look like. For a child, it was transportive, transformative, and planted a seed that continues to grow to this day, as do the number of planetariums worldwide.

Now in 2009, there were nearly 3,000 planetariums all over the world, mainly in developed countries. About 83 percent of the world's population and more than 99 percent of the U.S. and European populations live under light-polluted skies.[13] Though there is a correlation between the number of planetariums and population centers' density, it would not be prudent to create a false equivalency that as light pollution and lack of visibility of stars increase, so does the number of planetaria that are built.

Visiting a planetarium is a form of astrotourism, albeit vicariously, as people in developed countries have lost their ability to see the stars in any meaningful way. This is what is available to city dwellers and a far less expensive alternative to traveling hundreds, if not thousands, of miles to enjoy and relish the embracing cloak of a dark night sky. According to Loch Ness Productions, these virtual stargazing trips are quite popular; a company specializing in cosmically creative content for dome theaters, 146,974, 275 people visit planetaria each year. Only one percent of these ticket buyers represents nearly 1.5 million potential astrotourists.

It is overlooked and understated how quickly light pollution has stolen our view of the night sky and its impact on our collective psyche. As a student of astrotourism, it is important to understand the why behind this segment of the travel market and how it is born of a societal, environmental, ecological, and technological crisis. The common dictum, "You do not know what you do not know," is precisely applicable to light pollution and how it keeps people from knowing what exists in a dark sky.

If people are born and live their entire lives in metropolitan areas under a dome of light, where the stars are washed out by artificial lighting, then they will remain ignorant about what exists beyond the dome, not unlike the character in The *Truman Show*. They will never know what they are missing until they are exposed to it. To that end, a classic cult movie, *Soylent Green*, made in 1973, will be offered as an illustration.

Soylent Green is set in an overpopulated, impoverished, and polluted dystopian future of 2022. It was strikingly prescient in 1973, even if it was somewhat exaggerated. One of the characters, Sol, played by Edgar G. Robinson, opts for assisted suicide at a government clinic in a process referred to as "Going Home." Part of the euthanasia program has 20 minutes to watch Earth's movies when nature was still thriving and unfettered by pollution. Sol sees pastoral images of animals in the wild, flocks of birds, and a sky full of clouds, sunsets, and the raw beauty of a natural world for the first time in his life. His friend, Thorn, played by Charleston Heston, breaks into the euthanasia room. He had been watching the same movie as his dying friend; confused and overwhelmed by the images, he exclaims, "How could I know? How could I, how could I ever imagine?" The look of utter reverence, awe, and astonishment is conveyed in their eyes, and the parallel of today is nothing short of chilling on two levels.

When people, who have lived under city lights for their entire lives, see the Milky Way galaxy and a starry night sky for the very first time, they are overwhelmed and have an emotional response that is foreign to them. In that instant, their reality has changed. Once given a glimpse of the cosmos, their world-view is upended. It is an enlightening moment where they are literally dumb-struck and rendered speechless. It can be described as a spiritual, sacred, or mystical experience.

In researching this book, several stories came to light on how people introduced to a dark starry sky are brought to tears for the first time. It might be from the sheer majesty that is a night sky or the grief of knowing what has been missing in their life for all that time or from a mystical experience. There is hardly a tourist experience that elicits such a primal response as weeping. Bearing witness to a starry night sky for the first time can change people's lives.

The other level, which is extremely alarming, is this is what our world has become. A natural resource that once was accessible to all of us, a view of the universe we live in, is now a thing of the past and available only to those who can afford to travel to, or live in, a dark sky location. Like Harding escaping London's soot-choked air to experience the fresh air of the countryside in the 19th century, we find ourselves escaping the light-polluted skies to experience the night in the 21st century.

Light pollution is a global issue. Most of the world is affected by this problem, and humanity has enveloped our planet in a luminous fog of light that prevents most of Earth's population from having the opportunity to observe the soul-stirring splendor of a pitch night ignited with thousands of stars. This potentially has a consequential impact on indigenous cultures (and people in general) of unprecedented magnitude. Our biosphere has changed due to ALAN, and our connection to the rest of the universe has been ruptured.

If we think of indigenous people whose traditions are tied to the migration of certain species, and when that source of food is severely limited or disappears altogether, there is a detrimental impact on cultures. It is not just people's bodies that starve, but their hearts and souls as well.

CHAPTER 5

Where–When–What

As a child, I was afraid of the dark, but as an adult, I learned
that some of the best times in my life were when the lights were out.
—The Author ("foolosopher")

- Airbnb sees strong growth in travel linked to astronomical events and destinations known for stargazing. The year 2017 had more than 50,000 Airbnb guests from 26 countries who traveled to the United States for the solar eclipse. There are nearly 3,000 homes listed on the platform offering telescopes.
- One participant on Airbnb, Maria Elena, Cabo San Lucas, lists this way: "I will show the major constellations of the season, asterisms, planets, and travel beyond the solar system with a powerful telescope. The stars will tell the Mayan, Aztec, Greek stories and knowledge of the sky. I will show you how to read the sky wherever you are. You will look at the night sky in a meaningful way."

From a total solar eclipse to the Milky Way to the Northern Lights, many experts at the 2019 *Internationale Tourismus-Börse* Berlin, marketed as the world's leading travel trade show, were making a case for astronomical experiences. According to Andreas Haenel, astronomer, and director of the planetarium museum in Osnabrück, Germany, "Astrotourism is really an increasing business. We now see many travel agencies which offer this kind of tourism." Two questions that are particularly important to astrotourism are "where to go?" and "when to go?"

The When

The when to go is any time of the year when clouds are not dominating the sky, but some astronomical events occur that are "superstars" and compel the public to travel. Considerable numbers of people are interested, and prime spots may be booked years in advance. Certain months present unique events, like meteor showers that are loosely bracketed by calendrical dates and approximate times.

Total solar eclipses occur at precise moments that are calculated to the second, with a path on earth that requires the viewer to be at an exact place at an exact time. During the eclipse, the shadow of the moon tracking across the earth can move at speeds from 1,770 km/h at the equator to 8,046 km/h at the poles, with the shadow of totality only 267 km across.[1]

Viewing conditions change with the seasons, and gear to ensure the astrotourist's comfort will be needed. The best sky for viewing is during the winter. The Earth's atmosphere is not as hazy then because cold air has less capacity to hold moisture; the air is drier and clearer than in the summer months. Certain times of the month are better for stargazing due to the moon's waxing and waning rhythm. The days closer to the new moon are more advantageous, as the stars are more visible when not competing with the sun's reflection off the lunar surface. The ideal time to see the stars is after the moon has set or before it rises. This will change monthly, as the moon rises about 50 minutes later every day.

The What

The stars themselves and the accompanying nocturnal neighbors are topics that can fill volumes of books. The Milky Way galaxy will be the first and foremost object in the sky that your guests will be introduced to. Anecdotal evidence has shown that people who have never seen it think it to be pollution in the sky. Get familiar with the brightest stars and asterisms in the sky as they are ways to locate constellations. In descending brightness Sirius, Canopus, Rigil Kentaurus, Arcturus, Vega, Capella, Rigel, Procyon, Achenar, and Betelguese. Use the common asterisms of the Big Dipper, Cassiopeia, Orion's Belt, The Hyades, the Great Square of Pegasus, Orion's Sword, to get familiar with the night.

The Andromeda galaxy can be seen with the naked eye, appearing like a fuzzy patch in the Great Square of Pegasus, and with a good pair of binoculars or a modest telescope it is possible to see several galaxies.

The Satellites

According to the Union of Concerned Scientists, there are about 6,000 satellites in orbit as of January 2021, with 60 percent defunct and nothing more than space junk, with 2,666 operational. Over the coming decade, the Euroconsult estimates that there are 990 satellites launched every year. By 2028, there could be 15,000 satellites in orbit.[2] They crisscross the sky 24/7 but are most visible during the early evening and the pre-dawn hours as that is when they are reflecting the sunlight high in our atmosphere while the surface of the earth is wholly in the shadow. The best way to spot a satellite is to lay on your back and allow your eyes to relax to take in a full peripheral view of the sky; try to look at all of the stars simultaneously, and by doing so, you can tell one of them is moving. That will be a satellite and will be moving much faster than a high-altitude jet plane and will be utterly silent.

The Planets

The word planet comes from the Greek word *"planetes"* meaning wanderer. They traverse the ecliptic, an imaginary plane containing the Earth's orbit around the sun. The sun's path through the sky is the ecliptic, and all the planets and the moon follow closely to that path with a slight variance but with different speeds. Venus is the brightest appearing as an evening or morning "star" as it outshines everything else save the moon. Jupiter is more brilliant than many stars in the sky, as is Saturn, whereas Mars and Mercury are harder to see, with the latter a rare sight. Many phone apps will help you pinpoint the planets as they process across the night sky.

The Moons

Stargazers consider moonlight an impediment to viewing, as it diminishes the ability to see the starlight. However, the innovative proprietor of astrotourism products, the full moon (and the nights on either side of it), can easily be the main attraction that will lure people from metropolitan areas. People who live under ALAN have forgotten or never experienced an evening in the countryside, bathed by the light of a full moon. It has a universal appeal to all ages and cultures. For couples, it is all at once magical and enchanting while being romantic and dreamy.

Without the stars taking the night's attention, the moon provides lovers the opportunity to be starry-eyed with each other. Children can cavort in a haunting and mysterious landscape without any need for artificial illumination. This is a particularly suitable time for ghost stories of werewolves, lunatics, and other night tales that raise the hackles and are linked to the lunar cycles.

Consider offering your guests a "moon menu," that is, a snack or feast designed to fit the theme of a particular moon. What can be more bewitching and captivating than a picnic under *la bella luna*? Instruct your guests to allow their eyes to adjust to the night's natural light, and once they do, they will see how a flashlight or lantern becomes a "spell-breaker" to the full moon's silver luminosity. Shadows are pronounced, as well as shapes and depth of field, and all that is missing is color—it is as if you are living in a black and white film.

> *Everyone is a moon and has a dark side they never show to anyone.*
> —Mark Twain (humorist)

Each month offers a different moon and provides a different theme upon which to create a unique experience. Consider offering a package of 12 events for a client that runs the course of a year, where all they need to do is show up. A theme, blankets, food, beverage, optical equipment, and storytelling are provided, all under the gaze of a swooning moon.

Many Full Moon names are unique to cultures worldwide, and there are more celebrations tied to the moon than to the stars. Their name can be affiliated with seasons or indicate when the plants are animals are active (i.e., Corn Moon when it is time to harvest, Flower Moon when blossoms appear in Spring). Names are logically tied to flora and fauna of the regions like New Guinea's Flying Fish Moon or Native American's Beaver Moon.[3]

The following moons are associated with the Northern Hemisphere and temperate zones:

January—Wolf Moon—Known for its howling wolves.
February—Snow Moon—Known for snow on the ground.

March—Worm Moon—Considered the last full moon of winter.
April—Pink Moon—Phlox, a pink flower, begins to bloom.
May—Flower Moon—April's showers bring May flowers.
June—Strawberry Moon—Wild strawberries start to ripen.
July—Buck Moon—Bucks begin growing antlers.
August—Sturgeon Moon—The season to fish for this.
September/October—Harvest Moon—Time to reap.
September—Full Corn Moon—Time to harvest corn.
October—Hunter's Moon—The game has fattened.
November—Beaver Moon—Beavers build dams now.
December—Cold Moon—Winter has arrived.

The finest viewing will be in an area with an unimpeded view to the horizon like an open meadow, field, or atop a hill, escarpment, bluff, plateau, or ridge—the more sky you can see, the better. Summer's warmer weather requires less gear to remain comfortable; however, heat rising from the earth creates turbulence in the atmosphere, which will distort the view of the stars and create the illusion that they are twinkling.

Another possible drawback during the summer months, especially in the western United States, is smoke from forest fires that can travel hundreds of miles. As our climate continues to change and fire seasons become longer and more severe, the risk of obstructive smoke will continue to be a potential impediment to stargazing. Winter's sky holds the easily recognizable constellations like Orion, Taurus, and the Pleiades, while the summer sky shows off Scorpio, the largest constellation in the Northern Hemisphere, and the Milky Way.

As the earth turns, the sky overhead will reveal both winter and summer constellations to the committed viewer, one who will remain awake long into the night or choose to rise in the wee hours of the morning, before the sun begins to lighten the sky.

The Meteors

These stellar "blink-of-an-eye" moments have the misnomer of being called falling stars or shooting stars when they are not stars at all. The renowned astronomer, Ptolemy, thought that the gods on Mt. Olympus caused shooting stars. The story goes that when the gods wanted to see what mortals were doing, they pried the skies apart, and the stars fell out. Mortals, thinking the gods were watching, offered up their wishes, thinking that if they could be seen, then they would surely be heard. Early Christians considered them to be rising or falling souls or angels, including babies falling to Earth to be born. Other cultures believed they were souls being released from purgatory, who could finally begin their ascent to heaven and eternal peace.

Though we know better, the stories have not lost their charm and still capture our imagination. Meteor showers and the date of their arrival remain mostly constant from year to year. These celestial events can be exciting and visually stunning, as they put on memorable shows. The meteor shower intensity will ebb and flow depending upon the orbit of the comets and their proximity to Earth.

Most meteoroids (what they are called before they enter Earth's atmosphere) are pieces of other, larger bodies that have been broken or blasted off. Some come from comets, others from asteroids; some even come from the moon or other planets. Scientists estimate that about 48.5 tons (44,000 kilograms) of meteoritic material fall on Earth each day![4]

Although meteors may be seen at any hour of the night, they are best seen in the hours between midnight and dawn, particularly when the moon is not visible in the sky. The tremendous friction of a meteor passing through the earth's atmosphere causes it to produce light and ultimately disintegrate before reaching Earth's surface.[5]

Some meteors are called Earth-grazing fireballs because they parallel the Earth's atmosphere and are more inclined to leave long trails that can linger for several seconds before they re-enter space. This phenomenon is not unlike how a rock skips across the surface of the water. A huge meteor of exceptional brightness is called a bolide, especially if it breaks up; these can be as bright as the planet Venus during the evening or morning sky.

These are spectacular events and incite yells and whoops over the typical "oohs" and "aahs" that accompany an evening of shooting stars—they are never forgotten. Approximately 40 different meteor showers occur every year that are visible in either the northern or southern hemispheres; some are visible in both. Once meteors hit the atmosphere, they become

Figure 5.1 ©*American Meteor Society 2015*

meteorites. Meteor showers are graded by the number seen per hour, which can range from two to 100.

Some of this space debris makes the news, and YouTube views can be in the millions. The Chelyabinsk meteor broke up over the city of Chelyabinsk, Russia, on February 15, 2013. The blast was stronger than a nuclear explosion, triggering detections from monitoring stations as far away as Antarctica. The shock wave that was generated shattered glass and injured about 1,200 people. Some scientists think the meteor was so bright it may have briefly outshone the sun.[6]

The International Meteor Organization creates a yearly calendar that indicates the peak dates of the meteor storms. This is an abbreviated list from their 2019 calendar. Learn more at amsmeteors.org

A full list can be found at the link provided in the endnotes.

Meteor showers are best viewed lying on one's back. Find an open field or hilltop and do not focus on any specific place in the sky. This is an exercise in peripheral vision, not forward vision. When peripheral vision is engaged, the eye does not perceive the depth of field. What one then sees appears to flatten, which is ideal when viewing a night sky. The objective is to see as much of the sky as possible. As this is an event that takes place over many hours, one can sky gaze comfortably with their necks straight.

Name	Date of Shower	Peak	Per Hour	Rating
Ursids	17 Dec–26 Dec	23 December	10	medium
Quadrantids	28 Dec–12 Jan	4 January	110	bright
Alpha Centaurids	31 Jan–20 Feb	8 February	6	bright
Lyrids	14 Apr–30 Apr	23 April	18	bright
Eta Aquarids	19 Apr–28May	6 May	50	bright
June Bootids	22 Jun–2 Jul	27 June	variable	bright
Southern Delta	12 Jul–23 Aug	30 July	25	bright
Alpha Capricornids	3 Jul–15 Aug	30 July	5	bright
Perseids	17 Jul–24 Aug	13 August	110	bright
Draconids	6 Oct–10 Oct	9 October	10	medium
Southern Taurids	10 Sep–20 Nov	10 October	5	bright
Orionids	2 Oct–7 Nov	22 October	20	bright
Northern Taurids	20 Oct–10 Dec	13 November	5	bright
Leonids	6 Nov–30 Nov	18 November	15	bright
Puppid-Velids	1 Dec–15 Dec	multiple	10	medium
Geminids	4 Dec–17 Dec	14 December	140	medium

"Like a bolt out of the blue,
Fate steps in and sees you through
When you wish upon a star,
Your dreams come true."

Leigh Harline—Ned Washington (songwriters)

The Auroras

The aurora borealis (Northern Lights) and the australis borealis (Southern Lights) are major attractions in the pantheon of celestial events. The aurora is a breathtakingly beautiful, if hard to predict, phenomenon occurring year-round.

> The sun's magnetic field goes through a solar cycle that is approximately 11 years in length. Giant eruptions on the sun, such as solar flares and coronal mass ejections (CME), also increase during the solar cycle. These eruptions send powerful bursts of energy and material into space, creating effects on Earth.[7]

This magnificent display of light, color, and motion is a top attraction for astrotourists but it requires traveling to the top or bottom of the planet. To see them with any regularity, the traveler must endure extreme environments. They are rarely seen in the lower 48 of the United States. The summer months are off-season for aurora chasers, as the upper latitudes do not experience total darkness.

Most displays occur in a band known as the *auroral zone*, which is typically 3° to 6° wide in latitude and between 10° and 20° from the geomagnetic poles.[8] "Our own planet has auroras 24 hours a day," says Jim Spann of the Marshall Space Flight Center, "and we can see them even in broad daylight." The trick, he explains, is picking the right wavelength. "If we look at Earth from space using an ultraviolet (UV) filter, we see there are auroras underway at all times. It is a beautiful sight."

NASA operates a spacecraft called the Advanced Composition Explorer (ACE) that provides near-real-time 24/7 continuous coverage of solar wind parameters and solar energetic particle intensities, referred to as "space weather." When reporting space weather, ACE provides a warning (about one hour) of geomagnetic storms that can overload power grids, disrupt communications on Earth, and present a hazard to astronauts.[9] Spaceweatheralerts.com is a subscription service that sends the user text messages about solar activity.

Knowing when this CME happens provides vital information to determine the timing of unparalleled celestial events. The astrotourist or anybody interested in the auroras will use these valuable tools, as they portend the arrival of a display. Mobile smartphones give each one of us the capacity to be a citizen scientist and know, not predict, when things will occur in the sky, as sure as Aurora is the Greek goddess of the Dawn.

Figure 5.2 "Aurora" Giovanni Francesco Barbieri 1621 Ceiling of Casino Ludovisi, Rome

Aurora borealis tours and resort/hotel destinations are located in Alaska, Canada, Iceland, Norway, Finland, Sweden, Lapland, Russia, and Greenland. The Aurora Australis tours occur in Argentina, New Zealand, Australia, South Georgia Island, Tasmania, and the South Pole. The chance of seeing the displays increases closer to the poles. Because there are no landmasses near the South Pole, the northern displays are more readily accessible and where the vast majority of vendors are established. At this writing, there are 114 listed tours on tourradar.com and range in price from $234 to $19,972.[10]

Tour packages may include visits to multiple cities, destinations, attractions, and part of the time on a cruise ship. The quality of the trip, in many cases, has everything to do with the guide and their knowledge of the terrain, both on terra firma and the sky overhead. As the aurora display takes place over vast areas, it is not beyond the traveler to simply step outside on a night to see when they have arrived at a suitable destination. Some tours are self-guided, and from reviews found online, it was clear that little was offered that could not be accomplished with a guide book, auto transport, and a sense of adventure. When the term "expert guide" is included in the tour package, it is the adventurer's responsibility to learn what metrics they are using to qualify themselves as experts. Seek out individuals who have degrees in astrophysics or astronomy or others who possess years of experience leading these kinds of tours.

Lodges and resorts listed as being located within the auroral oval do so because there is a greater likelihood of seeing at least one display. They will also advertise the lack of light pollution, as does Kangerlussuaq's town in Greenland. Few could have predicted 30 years ago that being in a location with no outdoor lighting and a clear sky would be a selling point to attract tourists.

Jussi Eiramo, the owner of *Kakslauttanen Arctic Resort* in Finland, had the vision to figure out a way to accommodate his guests to be comfortable in a warm bed to view the mesmerizing and thrilling spectacle that is the northern lights. From his idea, history was made, and after a few experiments with prototypes, he came up with the original glass igloo in 1999.

This type of accommodation's phenomenal popularity is since you can enjoy the northern lights from a toasty interior while it is –25 degrees outside.[11] Igloos were never part of the Finnish or Lapland culture but were built and used by the Inuit people of Alaska, Canada, and Greenland.

Glass igloo accommodations are available in Norway, Sweden, Iceland, and Greenland. The largest number are in Finland and Lapland, which also has the largest selection of glass hotels and transparent igloos from budget options to luxury premium accommodations.

There are over thirty glass resorts in Finland alone, situated mainly in the northern areas.[12] Most of the glass igloos are within the Arctic circle, and though the best time to see the northern lights is between August and April, some igloo villages are open all year for this unique overnight experience.

Figure 5.3 Photo Kakslauttanen Arctic resort

Figure 5.4 Photo Kakslauttanen Arctic resort

At the time of this writing, 59 locations offered glass igloos or structures with prominent glass features developed to provide comfortable surroundings and accommodations to the astrotourist who wishes to see the auroral displays. One tour operator advertises it this way:

"Our accommodation takes many forms including the *Aurora Bubbles* or glass igloos. These structures give you a distinctive location in which to sleep, ensuring you can enjoy warmth and comfort, all while providing that all-important sky view."

These see-thru igloos have heated glass to keep off the ice and snow and provide other amenities, including wood-burning fireplaces, saunas, and hot tubs.

Many of these resorts offer daytime activities. Dog and reindeer sleds and sleighs, snowmobiles, ice fishing, snowshoeing, and cross-country skiing are a few of the pastimes listed. One location calls itself "the home to Santa Claus" and has a Santa house, park, village, and post office. Though it is impossible to predict the aurora borealis, most resorts and hotels use alarm services and wake up the guests if the Northern Lights are visible.

The glass igloo has become a worldwide phenomenon spawning alternative; there are inexpensive bubble models available online under $1,000. These clear dome-shaped tents provide a stellar way to accommodate an astrotourist in climes that are not sub-zero.

Odds and Ends

There exist obscure astronomical sites that rarely get mentioned yet hold all of the marvel and wonder of the better-known celestial phenomenon.

Sundogs

When suspended ice crystals refract the sun's light, a sun dog appears about 22 degrees left, right, or on both sides of the sun based on the crystals' location. They can range from red to blue, with the former closest to the sun and the latter furthest away. They are also called mock suns or parhelion, a Greek word meaning "beside the sun."

Zodiacal Light

Before dawn breaks or after twilight ends, it is possible to see this curious site that appears as an eerie cone of light comparable in luminosity to the Milky Way but even more milky in its appearance. It will be seen in the east before dawn during late summer/early autumn and in the west at dusk in the late winter/early spring.

Green Flash

When the conditions are right, this rare sight can occur fleetingly at the moment of sunset or sunrise, where a green spot may appear, just above the upper rim of the sun.

Moon Halos

Somewhat familiar, moon halos occur under similar circumstances as a sun dog with ice crystals refracting the sun's light, creating a circle of light that is 22 degrees in radius, which can also appear with the colors of the rainbow. It is a reasonably accurate indicator of turbulent weather approaching.

The Where

There are places dark enough to see the wonders of the night sky the world over, but here we focus on the destinations that have created the infrastructure to service clientele. Astrotourism in New Zealand has shown dramatic growth. At the 2019 New Zealand Starlight Conference, the theme was "Towards a Dark Sky Nation." About 120 delegates from 17 countries attended the conference to discuss light pollution and the benefits of international accreditation as a dark sky nation. There are three dark sky areas in New Zealand, one of which, the Mackenzie Basin, attracts about 150,000 astrotourists each year. Most of these visitors come from overseas, making dark-sky tourism in Mackenzie one of the country's biggest tourist attractions.

The website, spacetourism.space, has links to over 75 astro-destinations on every continent. These lodgings advertise the size and number of telescopes available for guest use, the clarity of their night skies, various amenities and activities, with accommodations ranging from rustic to chic. One location in Chile provides a telescope and retractable dome roof for each room, another lodge incorporates their wine cellar as part of the package, while others present nighttime programs led by local astronomers. Many of these astro-destinations are positioned near designated areas to provide accommodations and additional viewing opportunities. It is just outside these certified areas where the greatest growth potential may occur.

The IDA was founded in 1988, and its mission is to: *Preserve and protect the nighttime environment and our heritage of the dark skies through environmentally responsible outdoor lighting.* They are recognized as the authority on light pollution and the leading organization combating it worldwide. Specific criteria were created by the IDA that would appropriate an area to become a certified destination; the first one was Natural Bridges, Utah, in 2006.

The number of IDA certifications (and certifications from Fundaçion Starlight) is increasing at an accelerating rate, reflecting the growth of the astrotourist market. Communities, counties, states, and countries reap the certification benefits; it attracts tourist dollars, media coverage, and goodwill. These designations can take up to two years to obtain and require research, grassroots participation, local business, and government support. There are different distinctions, each with its own specific measurements, that must be achieved to gain certification.

Designations

Parks

Parks are publicly or privately owned spaces protected for nature conservation that implement good (dark sky friendly) lighting and provide dark sky programs for visitors.

Communities

Communities are legally organized cities and towns that adopt quality outdoor lighting ordinances and undertake efforts to educate residents about the importance of dark skies.

Reserves

Reserves consist of a dark "core" zone surrounded by a populated periphery, where policy controls are enacted to protect the core's darkness.

Sanctuaries

Sanctuaries are the most remote (and often darkest) places in the world whose conservation state is most fragile.

Developments of Distinction

Dark Sky Friendly Developments of Distinction recognize subdivisions, master-planned communities, and unincorporated neighborhoods and townships, where planning actively promotes a more natural night sky but does not qualify them for the IDA Community designation.[13]

Communities and Developments of Distinction are crucial when it comes to protecting the core of a reserve. Examples are Sun Valley and Ketchum's cities, Idaho, where outdoor lighting ordinances protect the core of the Central Idaho Dark Sky Reserve.

As remote regions recognize the potential to develop this sustainable form of tourism, they may take the necessary steps to gain certification. One can wait for empirical data to deliver statistical trends or engage in critical thinking and deductive reasoning to come to conclusions. Developing countries will continue to contribute more ALAN, further threatening their dark skies, an already rapidly diminishing resource. For the astrotourism industry to flourish, those on the supply side would be well-served to get involved in dark sky advocacy to protect the natural resource from which they intend to profit. To preserve and protect from the pressures of development, the vendor must be aware that sky glow from cities can travel up to 200 km, which has a deleterious effect on the very thing that will be attracting clientele—a dark sky.

"[There is] an emerging astrotourism trend as Airbnb sees strong growth in travel linked to astronomical events and destinations known for stargazing. In 2017, more than 50,000 Airbnb guests from 26 countries traveled to the US for the solar eclipse."[13] As of this writing, there are 78 IDA Dark Sky Parks globally, most of which (55) are located in the United States. There are three in Hungary; two in Germany, England, Scotland, Croatia, and the Netherlands; one in Spain, South Korea, Wales, Australia, Denmark, Japan, Israel, Ireland, Taiwan, and Australia. One IDA Park straddles an international boundary between the United States and Canada, demonstrating that all nations of the world have something in common, the night sky above them.

There are only 13 Dark Sky Reserves worldwide with three in the United Kingdom and France, two in Germany, and one in Wales, New Zealand, Ireland, Canada, France, Namibia, Australia, and the United

States. There are 10 Dark Sky Sanctuaries with three in the United States, two in New Zealand; one in Chile, South Africa, Australia; and a British Overseas Territory, the Pitcairn Islands.[13]

Airbnb and other online "owner to guest" platforms are uniquely positioned to propel astrotourism, as this niche market is a boost to local economies. International hotels and lodging chains are not well-situated to benefit from this new travel market, as dark sky destinations are spread out over remote areas that are not usually situated near other attractions.

> Through the Office of Healthy Tourism, we will foster initiatives that drive economic growth in communities, empower destinations from major cities to emerging destinations, and support environmental sustainability. Airbnb's local, authentic, people-powered travel ensures that more people can harness the benefits as more people travel. Astrotourism is an environmentally-friendly, authentic and sustainable way to travel to empower lesser-known, rural communities economically. At Airbnb, we are proud to be boosting this phenomenon thanks to hosts who share their home or passion for astronomy on the platform.[14]

Begun in 2008, Airbnb has decisively changed the travel market, giving locals around the world the opportunity to participate and prosper from the tourism industry. Table 5.1 is data collected by Airbnb and the Starlight Foundation. Airbnb has been tracking astrotourism trends and homeowners around the world who are hosting these stargazing enthusiasts. These numbers are substantive proof that astrotourism is an accelerating market, with some impressive growth in regions that have been overlooked. Expect to see more lodging, services, and other amenities developed for tourists traveling to see IDA/Starlight Foundation dark sky-designated areas. The Starlight Foundation has their own designations for hotels, cottages, restaurants, camps, and stellaries, as well as parks, reserves and tourist destinations. The following table was collected by the Starlight Foundation who provided Starlight Sites, and potential Starlight Sites, to perform this analysis with Airbnb.

Table 5.1 **This chart shows country, location, annual growth rate and nationalites visiting**

Country/state	Night sky area	Annual growth rate (%)	Top nationalities visiting
Kaposvár, Hungary	National Park of Zselic	105	Hungary, Germany, Netherlands, Great Britain, Austria
Bagnères-de-Bigorre France	Pic du Midi	99	France, Spain, Great Britain, USA, Netherlands
Gilbert, USA	Gilbert Riparian Preserve	164	USA, Canada, Great Britain, Mexico
Olijato, USA	Natural Bridges National Monument	70	USA, France, Spain, Germany, Italy
San Felipe, Mexico	National Astronomical Observatory	191	USA, Mexico, Canada, Germany, Spain
Windhoek, Namibia	Namibia	162	South Africa, Germany, USA, Namibia, France
Kailua-Kona, Hawaii USA	Mauna Kea	68	USA, Canada, Australia, Japan, Germany
Ouarzazate, Morocco	Atlas Mountains	52	France, Germany, USA, Great Britain, Netherlands
Yarmouth, Nova Scotia	Acadian Skies & Mi'kmaq	221	USA, Canada, Great Britain, Germany, Australia
Kiruna, Sweden	Campalta	134	Sweden, France, Germany, USA, China
Évora, Portugal	Alqueva Region	64	France, Portugal, USA, Canada, Spain
Lake Tekapo, New Zealand	Lake Tekapo	223	China, Australia, New Zealand, Singapore, USA
La Palma, Spain	La Palma Island	90	Spain, Germany, Great Britain, France, Switzerland
Antofagasta, Chile	Mano del Desierto	327	Chile, Argentina, USA, Germany, Brazil

CHAPTER 6

Space Tourism

Non est ad astra mollis e terris via

There is no easy way from Earth to the stars.
— Seneca the Younger (philosopher/statesman)

This little-known expression is from the play, *Hercules,* the fifth largest constellation in the sky. It is notably relevant for a chapter on Space Tourism, as getting into space is a heavy lift.

Technology changes tourism. During the age of sail, it took two to three weeks to travel from California to Hawaii. In 1866, Mark Twain visited Hawaii. He embarked from San Francisco and the steamship, *Ajax,* delivered him to the island chain in seven days. In 1936, 70 years later, passengers could fly from San Francisco to Hawai'i in 18 hours. The aircraft was a Flying Boat capable of taking off and landing on water. It was nicknamed the "*China Clipper.*"[1] They were named after another new piece of technology from an older time, the *Clipper Ship,* which got its name by dramatically "clipping" the time of ocean passage, in the 19th century. With today's aircraft, the trip from Los Angeles to Honolulu is approximately five and half hours; the next technological advance will be suborbital point-to-point travel, with flights from London to Australia in one hour!

Another example of technology that changed tourism is the story of SCUBA (Self Contained Underwater Breathing Apparatus), which was co-invented by Jacques Cousteau and Emile Gagnan in 1943. It was a ground-breaking, or more aptly, a water-breaking device, that gave people the means to breath underwater. Another world, filled with exotic and remarkable creatures, was now open for exploration.

Seventy-five years later, the active number of SCUBA divers worldwide is nearly nine million people. According to the Professional Association of Dive Instructors, an estimated 4,000 dive centers are operating across the planet. Wholesale dive gear sales alone (excluding revenue generated by dive boats, dive tours, dive resorts, etc.) account for $750 million worldwide. Tourism targeting divers and astrotourism are similar in that they are both impacted by the effects of human development: as the rise of ocean temperatures is bleaching coral reefs, so, too, are dark nights bleached by sky glow.

Today we are on the brink of another tourism explosion due to technological advances. *Star Trek* characters Captain James T. Kirk and Jean Luc Picard say at the opening of every episode, "Space, the final frontier;" it might well be the final tourist destination.

In 1958, the National Aeronautics and Space Administration (NASA) was responsible for a civilian space program that included aeronautics and aerospace research. A name had to be created for the people going into space. Reaching back to ancient Greece, NASA came up with the word "astronaut," which is a combination of the Greek words *Astron* for "star" and *Naut* for "sailor."

In 1961, Yuri A. Gagarin, a Russian cosmonaut, was the first man in history to travel into space and orbit planet Earth.[2] The FAI (Fédération Aéronautique Internationale) has designated the boundary of space, the Kármán Line, at 100 km above the earth. Using this criterion, as of April 9, 2020 over 500 people from 41 countries have gone into space. Of those space travelers, eight completed suborbital space flight, 550 reached Earth orbit, 24 slipped the bonds of our gravity well enough to travel beyond Earth's orbit, and 12 walked on the moon. Space tourism will increase this number, but it will only be available to the very affluent; ticket prices start at over $100,000.

In the 1960s, the world would tune their television sets to watch rockets travel into space, yet today these launches have become so common the public rarely notices them. If the event is momentous, like a trip to Mars or a private company launching people into space (i.e., SpaceX launching two NASA astronauts into space on May 30, 2020), media coverage will attract interest. In 2019, there were 102 orbital launch attempts worldwide, with 97 of them reaching orbit.[3] A website schedule of all launches worldwide can be found at spaceflightnow.com.

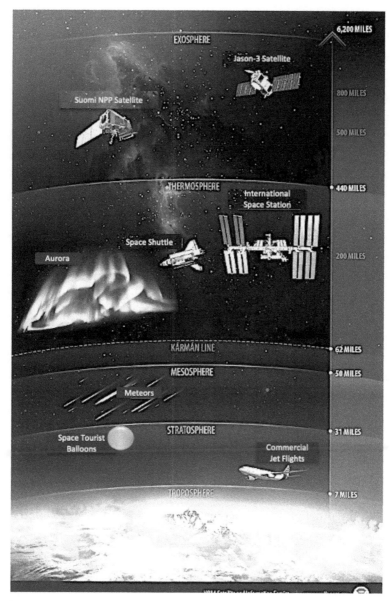

Figure 6.1 Comparing the altitudes of flying craft

The term astrotourism has been used interchangeably with space tourism, which has created confusion. From the author's perspective, astrotourists travel to a location to look up, and space tourists travel to a location to look down. A selection of space trips is currently available, and others are not far in the future. Space tourism will consist of suborbital flights, orbital flights, escape velocity trips, and staying at a low orbit spaceport. Escape velocity trips will take travelers beyond Earth's gravity grip and allow passengers to travel to the moon. Some alternative options are the "not quite space" trips that take people aloft to 30 km—well below the Kármán Line, but high enough to see the earth's curvature.

A quick lesson in gravity is necessary, as it plays an important part in space tourism's pricing. Imagine an enormous hoop, and inside the hoop is stretched a piece of elastic fabric. Put a baseball on the fabric, and it will make a dent. Replace it with a bowling ball, which has more mass, and the dent will be wider and deeper than the baseball. That dent is a gravity well. Any object with less mass will fall toward the heavier object and into the gravity well. Escape velocity speed is 11.19 km/s or 40,226 km/h. Costs would undoubtedly be calculated by how much fuel is necessary to climb out of that well and break free from our planet's gravitational pull.

Presently, the entire space economy—including rockets, communications, imagery, satellites, and crewed flights—does not exceed $100 billion, which is less than 0.1 percent of the global economy. In contrast, during the dot-com bubble in the late 1990s, companies' total capitalization amounted to more than 5 percent of global GDP.[4]

The Agents

The following are intermediaries who have developed relationships with companies conducting the launches and designing the technology that will take people heavenward. Virgin Galactic already has a customer admission model with Virgin Airlines and will create their own in-house ticketing, whereas SpaceX will use outside agencies to broker their trips. Some options include both participatory and observational excursions.

Space Adventures—Tysons Corner, Virginia, and Moscow, Russia

Space Adventures, founded in 1998 by Eric C. Anderson, brokers trips for orbital spaceflight missions to the International Space Station (ISS), circumlunar missions around the moon, zero gravity flights, cosmonaut training programs, spaceflight qualification programs, and reservations for future suborbital spacecraft. They booked passage for Denis Tito in 2001, the first tourist to pay his own way into space. For a reported twenty million dollars, Space Adventures reserved Tito a seat on a Russian built Soyuz rocket that ferried him to the International Space Station, where he spent about eight days in orbit.

In 2002, Tito spoke at the National Air and Space Museum in Washington, D.C. and referred to his trip as "the best eight days of my life." NASA had a long-running opposition to his flight, including preventing him from training with his Russian crewmates at the Johnson Space Center, which triggered a minor international incident. He believed that in the longer term, within the next 30 years, it would be possible to reduce the cost of orbital missions from $20 million to a few million dollars.

Reducing costs would require developing a reusable launch vehicle that could lower the cost of space access.[5] In less than 20 years, reusable rockets are now a reality being implemented by SpaceX and Blue Origin. At the time of this writing, the quote from Space Adventures for orbital space flights over the next several years starts at $50 million. Many factors impact pricing, including the year of launch, mission duration, and the mission profile.

Space Adventures has an agreement with Elon Musk's SpaceX to take tourists into space by 2022 aboard the Crew Dragon capsule. The plan is to blast off at pad 39A at NASA's Kennedy Space Center in Florida, where Apollo and Space Shuttle missions were once launched. These flights will take tourists into a high orbit and provide a view of the earth seen by the Gemini and Apollo astronauts.

Boeing is now testing the CST-100 Starliner, which will also be part of NASA's Commercial Crew Program; NASA will not own these spacecraft. In 2010, Space Adventures signed an agreement with Boeing to offer the unused seats on its Starliner to private citizens. It also books trips to Russia's Star City to witness Soyuz rocket launches and re-entries.

Axiom Space—Houston, Texas

Their team has deep NASA experience and announced their plans to launch a team ferried by SpaceX Crew Dragon to live aboard the ISS.

It will carry a company-trained commander and three private citizens. This mission will be the first fully commercial orbital space flight by non-government astronauts. Each passenger will pay $55 million[6] for an eight-day adventure in low-earth orbit. Even with the rate of inflation taken into account, this is more than twice as much as Tito's ticket when ferried to the ISS in a Soyuz rocket in 2001.

Space Affairs—Bremen, Germany

Space Affairs has been in operation for 20 years and is collaborating with the Yuri A. Gagarin Cosmonaut Training Center (GCTC) in Star City, Russia, offering opportunities to participate in various training kinds that relate to space travel. The participant can go through a cosmonaut "boot camp" to determine if they have the mettle to endure space travel stresses and rigors. There is both a physical and a psychological component of discovering one's suitability for this kind of tourism, as space is a life-threatening place. On their website, they pose the question regarding the training, "Do you have the 'Right Stuff,'" which is a salute to Tom Wolfe's book-turned-movie, *The Right Stuff,* about the early days of the U.S. space program.

The observational package allows the astrotourist to watch a Soyuz capsule reentry as it lands on the Kazakhstan steppes. It is a two-day excursion that costs $7,719.40 (or €6500) per person for a group with no fewer than five participants. The company also has plans to offer orbital space flights and "not-quite space" trips in their *Bloon,* a high-altitude balloon capsule that travels 36 km above the earth and provides a viewing distance that allows somebody to see Rome and Paris at the same time.[9]

August 2020, the quote from Space Affairs for flights to the ISS (which includes qualification, training, flight, ISS stay, and recovery) will be between $50 million for a Soyuz mission and $65 million for a Falcon/SpaceX mission. Prices will vary based on the mission profile and schedule. There are multiple companies offering weightlessness trips without the expense of going into space.

Before NASA could send people into space, it was necessary to determine the effects of zero gravity on the human body and mind. Fritz and Heinz Haber first suggested creating weightlessness in 1950 and became essential astronaut training for NASA's Reduced Gravity Research

Program. What was once exclusive to those traveling to space is now available to anyone who can afford a ticket. The participant experiences the sensation of being in zero gravity inside a fixed-wing aircraft that is flying in a series of parabolic arcs. The bigger the arc, the more time in zero-G; G is the gravity force at the earth's surface. A 2-kilo object experiencing two *gs* would weigh 4 kilos.

The unofficial nickname of the kinds of aircraft used for a weightless experience was the "Vomit Comet," as people experienced nausea in a weightless atmosphere. Nevertheless, why call it a "comet" other than it rhymes? The backstory is the British DeHavilland company was the first to manufacture commercial jets, moving away from propeller-driven technology; these new aircraft were called the "Comet." It traveled more than 160 km faster than any propeller craft, so the name was fitting. It was the first production commercial jet airliner that went into service in 1952 and held the distinction of being the first pressurized aircraft.[7] Because of DeHavilland's innovations, the groundwork was laid, and the technology developed would allow space exploration and high altitude flying.

One company, Incredible Adventures, has a location at the Aurora Aerospace Flight Center at the St Pete-Clearwater International Airport in Florida. They offer "zero-G" flights in a Commander 700 turboprop plane. The guest experiences about 10 seconds of weightlessness over the course of 10–12 parabolic flight maneuvers, for a total of about two minutes of zero gravity; it can accommodate one to two people.

Another grander version is on a modified Russian-built IL-76 MDK, a commercial freighter for outsized or heavy items. It is the largest parabolic plane globally and can host 11 passengers, providing weightlessness for about 28–30 seconds over the course of 10–20 parabolas.[8] There is a moment of enhanced gravity in both vehicles when you are feeling 1.8 g-forces as the aircraft is at a 45° angle going up or down. In Europe, the Air Zero G company has been organizing gravity-free flights for 30 years, taking people skyward in a Novespace Airbus A310; it is advertised as having the largest passenger capacity of any aircraft provide this experience.

The Launchers

These companies have developed and operate the hardware for transporting tourists into near or outer space.

Space Perspectives—Kennedy Space Center, Florida

Space Perspective is led by a team of professionals that have developed or operated all human balloon flights to the edge of space for the last 50 years. The team of Jane Poynter and Taber MacCallum that founded Space Perspectives also began World View, which uses high-altitude balloons to capture imaging for various business and government agencies. MacCallum and Poynter are the preeminent high-altitude balloon entrepreneurs in this research realm and, soon, tourism. Space Perspectives is one of the companies working to take balloon passengers to an altitude of about 30 km, where the darkness of space and the curvature of Earth are visible.

The company conducted a survey and found that roughly two million people would be interested in their balloon trips, potentially a market worth a quarter of a trillion dollars. Ticket prices have not been set, but company officials estimate the initial cost to be in the neighborhood of $125,000,[9] approximately half the price of a suborbital flight.

The balloon ascends, slowly lifting a pressurized capsule into the stratosphere, where passengers will have a two-hour excursion at cruise altitude before descending for a trip profile that lasts a total of six hours. The capsules are equipped with floor-to-ceiling parabolic windows and a glass viewing dome on the top of the capsule large enough to accommodate one passenger at a time. Their craft, the *Spaceship Neptune,* is undergoing testing at Cecil Spaceport in Jacksonville, Florida, in 2021.

Space tourism is set to create collateral jobs, as the company's president and CEO states, "Its [Space Perspectives] presence here in Florida creates not just job and supply chain opportunities, but opportunities for civilian astronauts to experience this planet Earth from the edge of space, a privilege previously available to only a few."[10] The company plans to build additional launch sites in Alaska, Hawaii, and internationally. To call their craft, a spaceship is taking artistic license, as one must pass the Kármán Line to enter into space; their balloon ascends only to 30 km. As this industry develops, it will be interesting to see how the intersection of space travel and marketing campaigns develop.

Virgin Galactic—Las Cruces New Mexico

Richard Branson founded Virgin Galactic (VG) in 2004, and the website reads, "Our mission, to be the Spaceline for Earth, means we focus on using space for a good while delivering an unparalleled customer experience." With the success of Virgin Atlantic Airlines (VAA), founded in 1984, the company would consider this venture a "spaceline" after running an airline. One big difference is VAA did not have to create new technology to go into business, so it has taken much longer for VG to get from square one to customer one. Their marketing campaign, One Small Step, allows interested future passengers to pay $1000 to get in line for a reservation. Stephen Attenborough, Commercial Director VG, says:

> We have been greatly encouraged by the ongoing and increasing demand seen from around the world for personal spaceflight. One Small Step allows us to help qualify and build confidence in our direct sales pipeline, as well as to ensure that those who are most keen to make reservations can do so at the earliest opportunity,

The next phase of the program, One Giant Leap, is expected before the end of 2020. Tickets will cost around $250,000, which is indeed a giant leap for most people's budgets. The naming of this adventure refers to man's first words on the moon, which need clarifying.

Neil Armstrong's most famous line—"That is one small step for man, one giant leap for mankind," uttered after becoming the first person to set foot on the moon—contained one small error that became one giant annoyance to the NASA astronaut. As Armstrong himself pointed out many times, the sentence is meaningful only if he says, "That is one small step for *a* man." He insisted that he said on July 20, 1969; otherwise, there is no distinction between a single individual and all of humanity.[11]

On December 17, 2018, VG executed a horizontal launch and flew the *VSS Unity* to an altitude of 364,000 feet, crossing the Kármán line. Since their first spaceflight, VG received 7,957 online reservation registrations in 14 months. The adventure is more than just the time aloft, as passengers must arrive at Spaceport, New Mexico, four days before the scheduled flight for medical checks, safety training, and G-force and microgravity simulation. Day four is launch day when six passengers climb aboard the *White Knight* for a horizontal take-off. Once the launch ship reaches altitude, it releases the spacecraft, which then fires jets for 63 seconds and ramps up to 4,319 km/h—three and one-half times the speed of sound.[12]

During VG's suborbital flights, customers will feel weightlessness for about four minutes. Gazing through windows that are 33 to 43 centimeters in diameter, passengers will be able to see the blackness of space beyond our atmosphere and the curvature of the earth. Six seats recline, a feature that will minimize the *g*-forces during the flight's boost and reentry phases. Seats come equipped with a screen that displays flight data and a personal communications system that gives passengers access to the pilots.[13]

VG's spaceships will not use parachutes or rockets to land but a new feathered reentry system that creates drag to slow the craft down, allowing it to glide back to earth to make a horizontal landing. This type of reentry system cannot be utilized for orbital space tourists, as going into an orbit necessitates traveling an additional 60 km from Earth's surface and will create higher reentry speeds. Burt Rutan, Spaceship One Designer, says:

> This is designed to be at least as safe as the early airliners in the 1920s, but do not believe anyone who tells you that the safety will be the same as a modern airliner which has been around for 70 years.

Under an agreement with NASA's Johnson Space Center, VG constructs a new orbital astronaut readiness program for private individuals interested in purchasing missions to the ISS.[14]

SpaceX—Hawthorne, California

Elon Musk began SpaceX in 2002, with the mission to "revolutionize space technology, with the ultimate goal of enabling people to live on other planets." Taking tourists aloft is an outlier for the company and not their main objective. SpaceX rockets broke long-standing barriers in their ability to repurpose, refuel, and reuse their rockets—ones that can lift more tonnage and return to earth than anything before now. They dubbed their rockets *Falcon 9* and *Falcon Heavy*, demonstrating how life imitates art, an homage to the *Millennium Falcon* in the *Star Wars* saga. The Falcon rockets will take the Dragon spacecraft (where passengers ride) into Earth's orbit, the ISS, and beyond. Japanese entrepreneur, Yusaku Maezawa, will become the aerospace company's first private passenger on a voyage around the moon that could happen as early as 2023.[15]

Blue Origin—Kent, WA

Jeff Bezos, the founder of Amazon and one of the richest men on the planet, started Blue Origin Federation in 2000, with the motto *Gradatim Ferociter,* Latin for "Step by Step, Ferociously." Unlike Elon Musk, Bezos had all the capital needed to create the technology to build living environments in space. The company was very secretive until 2015, when their capsule, the *New Shepard*, was launched to a height of 100.53 km and vertically landed under a parachute. By 2019, they had launched 11 times.

> Strapped into reclining seats at launch, *New Shepard* passengers will be able to unstrap and briefly float about the cabin near the top of the trajectory. They will experience a few minutes of weightlessness and enjoy panoramic views from the largest windows ever built for a spacecraft. As the capsule free falls back into the lower atmosphere, the passengers will experience about four to five times the normal pull of gravity during the initial stages of the plunge back to Earth.[16]

A person who weighs 68 kg will have the experience of weighing 340 kg. Our tolerance of *g*-forces depends not only on the magnitude and duration of the acceleration or deceleration but also on our body's orientation. We are most vulnerable to a force acting toward the feet because this sends blood away from the brain. Five to ten seconds at four to five Gs (vertically) typically leads to tunnel vision and loss of consciousness.[17] Seats are a key element to travelers' comfort and their ability to remain conscious.

Part of pre-flight training is to determine a tourist's capacity to withstand *g*-forces. Blue Horizons has not booked any passengers at this writing; however, they have established the *New Shepard* for suborbital flights and designed the *New Glenn* for orbital flights. These ships' names reflect the original flight profiles of the two astronauts, Alan Shepard and John Glenn, who were the first Americans to make those trips into space.

Space Ports

Plans are being laid by the Gateway Foundation to build a spaceport positioned in low-earth orbit and be capable of handling 200,000 visitors a year. According to their president, John Blincow, "The Gateway Foundation aims to build large rotating spaceports because by doing that you can create a true economy in low earth orbit that is economically self-sustaining." This will be the first commercial construction project in space, making real the presuppositions of Konstantin Tsiolkovsky, a science fiction writer who, in 1895, wrote about a rotating spaceport that used solar energy.

Gateway's wheeled design has been considered for over half a century, with Walt Disney and Werner Von Braun drawing up plans in the 1950s. Their Lunar Gravity Area (LGA) will consist of a large open-air gymnasium, a Japanese garden park, a food court, a restaurant, a casino, and a bandstand for concerts. A vertical, layered garden is planned for growing fruits and vegetables. Under the LGA floor will be a layer of sound-proof hotel rooms called the LGA Habitation Area. The LGA Habitation area is designed to save weight; each room will be simple yet elegant. The trip from Earth to Gateway's low-earth orbit will take about 24 hours.[18]

This is an unimaginably ambitious plan, yet very well within the capabilities of our expanding technologies. The Gateway Foundation anticipates having the ability to receive guests by 2027, with a construction time of just over 1,000 days. In the first half of the 21st century, science fiction will become astrotourism's reality and eventuality.

CHAPTER 7

Eclipse Chasers

No pessimist ever discovered the secret of the stars or sailed to an uncharted land, or opened a new doorway for the human spirit.
                                        —Helen Keller (author-activist)

The number one astrotourist event is a total solar eclipse. It towers above all other celestial phenomena, generating more press and temporarily relocating more people than any other event. Eclipse chasers and the tours that service them have been around for more than half a century. Paul D. Maley, the founder of Ring of Fire Expeditions, the longest consecutive astronomical tour organization in the United States, had this to share about the surge in interest.

> Astro tourism is on the rise. While I don't have specific proof in terms of numbers of people, the increase in wealth as people age show that most people 50+ are responsible for that increase with *Ring of Fire Expeditions*. Younger people, not so much since they are predominantly having to work. Since the August 2017 solar eclipse there has been a dramatic rise in inquiries from US eclipse watchers. Since the August 2017 solar eclipse there has been a dramatic rise in inquiries from US eclipse watchers. Our inquiries increased by 30% in the past 2 years. Increasing astrotourism has caused small towns to fill up faster and we now have to work 3–4 years in advance of every eclipse trip to verify we can get the space that before we could get in 1 year's advance planning cycle.

These "once-in-a-lifetime" events are really happening all the time but to view them literally requires chasing them down by traveling the globe. The last total solar eclipse that traversed the continental United States was in 2017 and it created substantive data that is being studied to forecast

what can be expected in 2024. According to Martin Knopp, an adminis-
trator at the Federal Highway Administration,

> Depending on weather and how many people are up for a Monday
> road trip, some two to seven million of them are expected to travel
> to that narrow zone on August 21, 2017—meaning travelers may
> experience some of the worst traffic jams in American history.

The days before and after the eclipse could see humans' greatest temporary mass migration to see a natural event in U.S. history.[1]

There is nothing else on the planet that moves so many people, figu-
ratively and literally, as a total solar eclipse. This singular moment in time
remains etched in a person's memory to the end of their days and drives
more people to astrotourism than anything else. Since North America's
2017 solar eclipse, interest in the wonders of the sky has skyrocketed.
Scott Dunn, an award-winning luxury tour operator, notes that bookings
for astro-experiences have recently tripled.

While it is hard to quantify how many travelers are stargazing in
dark sky spots and traveling to see eclipses, astrotourism (traveling for
astronomical experiences) is one of the top travel trends for 2019. In
2019, expect star-seekers to venture everywhere from Portugal's Dark Sky
Alqueva Reserve to Chile for a total solar eclipse set to occur on July 2,
2019, and January 3, 2019.[2] Looking back at the data from the 2017
eclipse, a great number of vendors, from souvenir stores, restaurants, and
mom-and-pop shops, to major hotel chains, all benefited from people's
curiosity about this rare astronomical phenomenon. There was a flood of
memorabilia manufactured and purchased. Even the United States Postal
Service celebrated the moment by issuing a heat-sensitive eclipse stamp.
When a finger touches the stamp, the shadow in front of the sun disappears, and the moon appears, complete with lunar surface detail.

Marriott International reported the total number of rooms booked
in 16 locations in the eclipse path was up 60 percent compared to the
previous year in those same locations. At one Hilton hotel located in
the totality path, which had not yet sold-out, rates started at $425.
For the previous week, the same room was available for $199.[3]

In 2017, it was estimated that 88 percent of American adults—about 215 million people—watched the solar eclipse, either in person or electronically. That is near twice the number of people that watched the Super Bowl that year. If the eclipse had been a television program, it would have garnered the most viewers of any in American history; the audience for the cosmic event was almost 18 times greater than the "Game of Thrones" finale a week later.[4]

This illustrates how astrotourism transcends many of the demographics and cultural differences among people, bringing them together under one roof—a roof with stars on its ceiling.

"What is most exciting about April 8, 2024, a total solar eclipse is that the total phase of the eclipse is nearly twice as long as the 2017 Eclipse," said Michael Zeiler, an eclipse cartographer.

This eclipse is going to be a much bigger deal than in 2017. While 12 million people in the United States lived within the path of the 2017 eclipse, 32 million people already reside within the path of the 2024 eclipse.[5]

The totality path will pass over some 15.2 million people who live in cities with populations of one million or more. As solar eclipses are the gateway into astronomy, it can be anticipated that a great number of people will whet their appetite and want to see more of a night sky replete with stars. "We calculate that even if 1% of the 12 million that live within the Path of Totality in 2017 finds a passion for eclipse chasing, that will effectively create a much larger audience," says Aram Kaprielian, International President at Travel Quest, who has seen over 20 total solar eclipses.

When the sky goes black in the blink-of-an-eye, it is as startling as anything a human can witness. No wonder the uninitiated thought the world was coming to an end, since night does not just fall, it slams shut. Our normal experience is witnessing the stars slowly appear, one at a time, over the course of twilight's last gleaming. It takes anywhere from 30 minutes to two hours, depending upon one's latitude, to descend from daylight into the darkness of astronomical twilight.

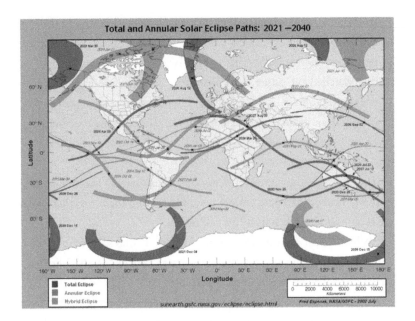

Figure 7.1 Charting eclipses 2021 to 2040

During a total solar eclipse, there is no twilight. All of the stars appear instantaneously, and the response is involuntary. One thing that can be said about astrotourism is that it fully exemplifies the expression, "Life is not about how many breaths you take, but by how many times your breath is taken away."

The 2024 Eclipse will be passing over multiple highly-populated cities. Many of the residents have never seen a starry sky due to the dome of light that hangs over many of our cities. Hopefully, millions of people will have the opportunity to see the stars, even if momentarily. However, if municipalities fail to shut down specific power grids, their photo-sensor street lights will come on during this fleeting nightfall. If a city's street lights come on, it will profoundly impact a total solar eclipse's full spectacle and look much like any other night.

Hopefully, the mayors of cities in the path of totality will follow the example of New York City in January 1986, dubbed "Halley's Comet Night," by then-New York Mayor Ed Koch. In all five boroughs, Koch had arranged for designated locations to temporarily extinguish their normally bright lights to allow New Yorkers to have a better view of this famous comet, which was low in the western evening sky. About 40,000 people gathered at Jones Beach, Long Island, to catch a glimpse of this once-in-a-lifetime event.

Compared to the "Great American Total Eclipse" of August 21, 2017, the 2024 eclipse will be far superior. The totality path will be roughly 40 percent wider, and the duration of totality along the centerline of the eclipse path will last anywhere from 42 to 107 seconds, longer than the maximum duration of the 2017 eclipse.[6] Because both the 2017 and 2024 eclipses passed and will pass, over both Makanda and Carbondale, Illinois, they are touting themselves as the place where the two center-lines cross, with Carbondale and its Southern Illinois University partner adopting the tagline, "Eclipse Crossroads of America."

The most advantageous place for observing is just outside Nazas, Mexico, where the centerline duration is 4 minutes and 28 seconds. Nowhere else will the eclipsed sun appear higher or totality last longer. These factors will almost certainly attract many amateur and professional astronomers and tour operators to Mexico, where good weather prospects are very encouraging. Indeed, Nazas is already being dubbed "Eclipse City." Its proximity to the point of greatest eclipse is mentioned on its Wikipedia page.[6] When the moon covers around 90 percent of the sun, the light will begin to fade dramatically to create an eerie, silvery atmosphere, and shadows become sharper. By standing under a tree and watching the sun's light filtered by the leaves, the viewer will see hundreds of tiny crescents of light on the ground. Punching a hole in the top of a take-out coffee cup or a piece of cardboard will serve the same purpose as the leaves. There is a rapid drop in temperature.

Spending the money on eclipse glasses is *essential to protect your eyes*, as they are indispensable to watch the moon passing over the sun's face before the moment of totality—this is *the only time you can look directly at the sun safely*. They can be found online, and links are listed in the Resource section of this book. An alternative method for safe viewing of the partially eclipsed sun is to cross the outstretched, slightly open fingers of one hand over the outstretched, slightly open fingers of the other, creating a waffle pattern. Facing away from the sun, look at your hand's shadow on the ground. The little spaces between your fingers, where the sun penetrates, will project a grid of small images on the ground, showing the sun as a crescent during the partial phases of the eclipse.

If past migrations to see a solar eclipse are any indication, all roads will lead to the path of totality in 2024. For 2019, one of the largest cities in the path of totality, San Juan, Argentina, was one of the most popular eclipse destinations. Its population of 112,000 was expected to quintuple on the days surrounding the eclipse.[7] Other than famine, war, or catastrophes, there is no single event on earth with more people migrating than to witness an eclipse. An estimated 130 million people will be positioned either inside or within less than a day's drive of the total eclipse zone.

The American portion of the total track of totality will average 184 kilometers in width and stretch from southwest Texas to northern Maine. There is every reason to believe that the 2024 event will surpass the number of people traveling in 2017, as there are larger population centers nearby. The big question is, "Where are people going to park?" It is not hard to imagine that traffic literally comes to a standstill during the moment of totality, as people will likely stop their car to look at one of the greatest celestial events of all time

Major metropolitan areas, like Pittsburgh, Memphis, St. Louis, Louisville, and Detroit, are only a few hours' drives from the path of totality. Even with Detroit's 99.4 percent partial eclipse, it is still not enough to create the conditions where the viewer can look directly at the sun.[8] Cultures from time's beginning have sought to explain solar

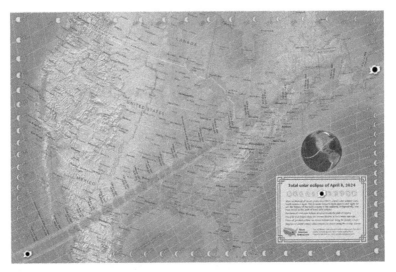

*Figure 7.2 **North American Eclipse 2024***

Source: Great American Eclipse.com

eclipses, and while some ancients could predict these events, others created tales that were totally void of science.

- The ancient Chinese did not believe a solar eclipse was simply the Moon covering the Sun; they determined a dragon was devouring it. This alarming consensus prompted them to clang pots, bang drums, and howl to frighten the dragon away.
- To the ancient Greeks, a solar eclipse meant the gods demonstrated their anger and signaling the start of earthly destruction.
- According to Choctaw legend, a mischievous black squirrel gnawing on the Sun is the cause of eclipses.
- Ojibwa and Cree's peoples have a story that a boy (or sometimes a dwarf) named Tcikabis sought revenge on the Sun for burning him. Despite the protestations of his sister, he caught the Sun in a snare, causing an eclipse. Various animals tried to release the Sun from the trap, but only the lowly mouse could chew through the ropes and set the Sun back on its path.
- According to ancient Hindu legend, a cunning demon named Rahu sought to drink the nectar of the gods and thus attain immortality. As punishment, the demon was promptly beheaded, and it is his decapitated head flying across the sky that darkens the Sun during an eclipse. His immortal head, in perpetual pursuit of the Sun, sometimes catches and swallows it, but the Sun quickly reappears, as Rahu has no throat.
- The Inca of South America worshiped Inti, the all-powerful Sun God. Inti was generally believed to be benevolent, but solar eclipses were understood to be a sign of his wrath and displeasure.[9]

The plans for the 2024 event are already underway. The solar eclipse of 2017 was not 24 hours old when the Maria International Travel Agency in Detroit started receiving calls for hotel and flight reservations for the areas in the path of the 2024 eclipse.[10] Being within the path of totality is better than being outside it, but some places within the path may be better than others, depending on preferences and budget. Experienced eclipse chasers aim to balance three factors: duration of totality, local accommodations, amenities, and attractions, and the likelihood of clear skies.[11]

CHAPTER 8

Ancient Monuments to the Stars

Two things fill the mind—the starry heavens above me and moral law within me.

—Immanuel Kant (philosopher)

Because astrotourism is a new field of travel, it continues to be defined; and what constitutes an astrotourist destination remains open to interpretation. Before the space age, there were no rocket launches to watch. As technology advances, the field of possibilities for today's astro-adventure traveler continues to expand.

In Valerie Stimac's recently published Lonely Planet guide, *Dark Skies: A Practical Guide to AstroTourism* (2019), research facilities are included, such as the Jet Propulsion Laboratory in Pasadena, California, or CERN (Conseil Européen pour la Recherche Nucléaire) in Switzerland. Just as the stars are best viewed using one's peripheral vision, so can the experience for the astrotourist be expanded by widening the field of vision. Like the space traveler, the astrotourist is an explorer who seeks new domains and locations to visit that are inextricably tied to the stars. From one perspective, it is not just about what happens in the sky but how what happens in the sky shapes humanity.

During their empiric reign, the Romans replaced *Helios* (the Greek sun god) with the Latin, *Sol*, a root word that continues to refer to the sun in the present day, as in the term "solar system."[1] Some of the human's greatest monuments, earthworks, and architectural creations are aligned with the stars—primarily the closest one, Sol. There is a new field of study called archeoastronomy, and it is described as such: "The study of ancient or traditional astronomies in their cultural context, utilizing archaeological evidence. The subject uses historical knowledge of our ancestors.

Archeoastronomy also uses monuments and written records to evaluate astronomical traditions. The importance of archeoastronomy is that it allows us to understand something about prehistoric times and astronomy knowledge that flourished."[2]

Archeoastronomy incorporates several sciences to create a picture of how ancient man tracked and studied the sky. As discoveries are made during digs, archaeology and anthropology are used to gain a comprehensive picture. It is also a historical and an astronomical undertaking, as archeoastronomy can be applied to all cultures and all time periods; the study and stories of the sky vary from culture to culture. Many of these places are heavily trafficked, like the Pyramids of Giza, Chichén Itzá, and Stonehenge.

We expand the definition of astrotourism, as these ancient monuments were designed, built, and intricately tied to celestial events. These monuments are an enduring embodiment of how many ancient civilizations knew about the stars and how much we continue to give them importance. Because astronomy is the oldest of our natural sciences, the practitioners were most likely revered and bore titles like the high priest, shaman, wizard, and magi (the origin of today's word magician). To those who do not understand the movement of the stars, the ability to predict the rains, the movement of migrating animals, the time to plant and harvest, and when it was time for people to fish and hunt is enigmatic arcane knowledge.

Today, thousands of years later, even with all of our science and understanding of the workings of the universe, learning how to identify the stars and constellations for the uninitiated remains almost esoteric in its undertaking.

Science is not only compatible with spirituality; it is a profound source of spirituality.

—Carl Sagan

This sense of wonderment is ripe for cultivation in this new field of tourism. This understanding was so potent and essential that enormous structures were built to measure the earth's subtle movements as it spun and wobbled back and forth on its axis. These megaliths are "bucket list" destinations that include various archeological sites around the world built with an astronomical correlation in mind by cultures that disappeared long ago. They are the keepers and markers of time over millennia; the astrotourist can stand in the same place, witness the same celestial phenomenon, and be part of a history that spans the ages.

The ancients understood that the equinoxes occur when the sun rose at due east and set at due west twice a year and that they were indicators of spring and fall. Watching the movement of our closest star, they could divide the year in a half. The solstices were known to be the longest and shortest days of the year. The equinoxes fell between those two astronomical events, the year now quartered. Between the equinoxes and solstices were cross-quarter days. These were the larger revelries of pre-Christian cultures: October 31, February 2, May 1, and August 2nd. These celestial celebrations persist to this day, but under different guises.

The ancients saw the season as heralded by the equinoxes and solstices but embodied and exemplified by flora and fauna six weeks later. An example is the spring equinox, which falls on March 21/22; in temperate zones, however, it is still wet and cold. Six weeks later into the season, temperate zones are in bloom, and spring is celebrated with May 1 festivities. Winter solstice falls on December 21/22, but the depth of winter is on February 2. Although Americans call this Groundhog Day and Catholics call it Candlemas, it originated with the Neolithic Celts named Imbolc (also called Brigid's Day). They knew it fell about halfway between the winter solstice and the spring equinox.

When these solar alignments occur at many of these megaliths, they are noted by the first rays of the sun passing through a portal, extending the length of a passageway, going through two towers, or even shining a light on a tomb deep underground. Many of these destinations are designated as UNESCO World Heritage sites, like Persepolis's ruins in Iran.

There has been speculation and debate over whether these ruins were a site for celebrating Nowruz, a spring celebration. According to Mary Boyce, a British scholar of Iranian languages and an authority on Zoroastrianism, "It seems a reasonable surmise that Nowruz, the holiest of them all, with deep doctrinal significance, was founded by Zoroaster himself." It begins at the spring equinox, the moment when the sun crosses the equator and day and night are of equal length. Described by 11th-century Persian astronomer and poet Omar Khayyam as "the renewal of the world," Nowruz dates back thousands of years[3] and is perhaps one of the oldest celebrations the planet.

Perhaps more important than winter or summer solstice is the vernal equinox, as it portends the beginning of new life and the survival of another winter. In conjunction with the International Astronomical Union (IAU), UNESCO has created a resource with an interactive map that links the cyber explorer to numerous sites worldwide, both ancient and modern. It can be found on UNESCO's *Portal to the Heritage of Astronomy* website.

The Megaliths

This is a limited list of megaliths and ancient monuments that could supplement the itinerary of an astrotourist who wishes to broaden the scope of their experience. The bracketed dates were when UNESCO designated these monuments a World Heritage Sites.

Newgrange, Republic of Ireland, circa 3200 BC [1993]

Newgrange is best known for the winter solstice sun illuminating its underground passage and burial chamber. Above the entrance to the passage of the mound is an opening called a roof-box. Access to the chamber on the solstice mornings is decided by a lottery, which takes place at the end of September each year.[4]

Pyramid of Giza, Egypt, circa 2550 BC [1979]

The Great Pyramid of Giza is nearly perfectly aligned along with the cardinal points—north, south, east, and west—with "an accuracy of better than four minutes of arc, or one-fifteenth of one degree."[5] An archaeologist has determined that Egyptians may have aligned the monument almost perfectly using the fall equinox.[6]

Chichén Itzá, México, 1000 CE [1998]

An international poll was taken in 2007 of more than 100 million people who voted this destination as one of the "New 7 Wonders of the World."

The late afternoon sun creates the illusion of a snake slithering slowly down the northern staircase on every equinox.[7] Video of this phenomenon can be found on YouTube.

Stonehenge, England, 3000 BC [1986]

There is an ongoing debate on Stonehenge's architecture and its meaning. In 1963 American astronomer Gerald Hawkins proposed that Stonehenge had been constructed as a "computer" to predict lunar and solar eclipses; other scientists also attributed astronomical capabilities to the monument. Many of these speculations have been rejected by experts,[8] but it does not diminish the popularity of this iconic site.

Maeshowe, Orkney, Scotland, 3000 BC [1999]

Considered Europe's finest chambered tombs and an extraordinary example of Neolithic architectural genius as it was designed and built to align with winter's solstice. The rays of the setting sun pierce the narrow passageway and traverse its length, illuminating a burial chamber inside.[9]

Uxmal, Yucatan Mexico, 600–900 CE [1996]

The Pyramid of the Magician had an alignment specific to Venus's movement in the sky and was a bellwether of the coming rains. A portion of the grounds was designated as a ball court, with a vertical hoop for a ball to pass through, not unlike basketball. The game had always been connected to mythical and cosmic themes, with the ball symbolizing the stars' movements.[10]

Chaco Canyon, New Mexico USA, 850-1250 CE [1987]

Chaco's major center of ancestral Pueblo culture is remarkable for its monumental buildings and its distinctive architecture. An ancient, urban ceremonial center may be found there that is unlike anything constructed before or since.[11] The two- to three-meter sandstone slabs at Fajada Butte in Chaco Canyon cast shadows of the morning and midday sun, which indicate both solstices and equinoxes on a spiral petroglyph.[12]

Of the 1,121 UNESCO World Heritage sites worldwide, Chaco is one of only 20 sites in the United States. Since 1991, the park has offered an astronomical program.

Karnak, Egypt, 2000 BCE [1979]

The Temple of Karnak is dedicated to the god Amun. During the solstices, the sun's rays pass through the entire temple's entire length and into a room devoted to this Egyptian deity.

Chankillo, Peru, 500–200 BC [2013 Tentative List]

The 13 towers of Chankillo, situated between two observation platforms, spanning the sun's entire annual rising and setting arc. Over the year, the sun's path gradually shifts along the horizon, passing over each tower. The inhabitants of Chankillo would have been able to determine the date, with an accuracy of two to three days, by watching the sunrise or sunset from the correct observation platform.[13]

Cahokia Mounds, Illinois, circa 800–1400 CE [1982]

This is the largest pre-Columbian settlement north of Mexico. It is the pre-eminent example of a cultural, religious, and economic center of the Mississippian culture. Situated there is an astronomical observatory, Woodhenge, consisting of a circle of wooden posts that marked the solstices and equinoxes.[14]

Machu Picchu, Peru, 1450 CE [1983]

Machu Picchu is among the greatest artistic, architectural, and land use achievements anywhere globally, making it the most prominent and tangible legacy of the Inca civilization.[15] There is a giant stone at the top of this sacred mountain, *Intihuatana*, which means "the place when the sun gets tied." It is positioned, so each corner sits at the four cardinal points (north, south, east, and west). As a result, the stone is a precise marker of the two equinoxes; at midday on the equinox, the sun is directly above the stone, creating no shadow.[16]

Mnajdra, Malta, 4000–3000 BCE [1980]

This megalith is an effective year-round calendar. During the equinox, the sun rises in perfect alignment with the main doorway; sunlight floods into the central corridor, traveling into the megalith to the innermost apse. The solstices are marked by the narrowest slivers of light that pass through the sides of the main doorway, shining onto the furthest edge of the apse.[17]

Angkor Wat, Cambodia, 1100 CE [1992]

Angkor Wat is one of the largest archaeological sites in operation in the world.[18] The builders of Angkor Wat created a reminder of the greater cosmic order, reflected in both the passage of time and in the changing rays of the sun. Angkor Wat encoded calendrical, historical, and cosmological themes into its architectural plan for the temple. The sun rises during equinoxes, perfectly aligned to the central and tallest tower in the complex.[19]

Hovenweep, Colorado-Utah Border, 1200 CE

The Ancestral Puebloan people may have used Hovenweep's towers as astronomical observatories, recording the seasonal wheel's turning for agricultural and ceremonial purposes. There is a portal at Hovenweep Castle that aligns to the equinox and points to the sunrise azimuth four days *after* the vernal equinox. This orientation was determined by halving the number of days between the winter and summer solstices.[20]

Mudumal, Telangana, circa 5000 BCE

This site probably holds the distinction of being one of India's oldest megalithic structures, dating back 7,000 years. In fact, archaeologists note that this is one of the rare sites where a star constellation depiction has been found. The site consists of 80 massive menhirs (tall upright stones) and about 2,000 alignment stones, making it one of the largest concentrations of menhirs excavated anywhere in India. The constellation depicted has been identified as Ursa Major.[21] Many cultures worldwide recognized a bear in that same grouping of stars, substantiating the interconnectedness we all have with the night sky.

CHAPTER 9

Sundials and
Astronomical Clocks

Una ex his erit tibi ultima.

One of these [hours] will be your last.

—Unknown

Astrotourism is a much greater field of exploration than viewing the night sky. Traveling to watch rocket launches or reentries is included in the current definition of this new segment of tourism, but that was not always the case. Astronomical tourism began in the 1940s and has expanded upon its definition as markets and technology advanced.

Places like Space Camp in Alabama, space-themed hotels, museums of astronomy weightlessness experiences, astronaut boot camps are being included as possible interests of the astrotourist. As science's pursuit of knowledge in the emerging fields of astrophysics, aerospace engineering, astrometry, astrogeology, cosmology, astrobiology, and archeoastronomy develop and expand, so will the possible opportunities for the astrotourist to consume.

Food tourism is well established and is augmented by the recent ascent of agritourism. Agritourism expands upon food tourism by bringing travelers to the source and providing options to participate in food production, harvesting, and working on a farm or ranch. Humanity's relationship with, and response to what transpires in the sky, can be part of the astrotourist's exploration.

We have measured the stars' movements for thousands of years, and the devices that track the motion of the heavens continue to advance as technology evolves. In the 14th century, time-keeping mechanisms were designed to measure the turn of the celestial wheel and did so with astounding accuracy. These astronomical clocks are still working—and in some places, the town's biggest attraction.

Sundials

A distinction made in this text designates a sundial as a "star clock." The nearest star, our sun, and Earth's position with it are used to tell time. Sundials are the earliest type of time-keeping devices. Time is determined using the sun's rays to create a shadow with an object (i.e., a stick) and track the shadow's path throughout the day. The oldest known sundial was found in Egypt and dates from Thutmose III, about 1,500 years BC. It held two segments of stone: one that held the needle and another marked to indicate the hours of the day.[1]

As the day progresses and the earth turns, the sun appears to travel across the sky, which causes an object's shadow to move; this is interpreted as the passage of time. The first object for indicating the time of day was probably the *gnomon* (Greek for "he who knows"), dating from about 3500 BC. For over 5,000 years, sundials (star clocks) were the standard for telling time. Until the 19th century, sundials were still used to reset mechanical clocks.[2] Using a star to tell time was so accurate, the entire population of a city set their watches to it.

> We may here remark that at Paris, and we also believe at Edinburgh (during the 18th and 19th century) and elsewhere, the hour of noon was at one time proclaimed by a cannon, which was fired by the rays of the sun concentrated on a magnifying glass so placed as to ignite the powder in the touch-hole when the sun reached its meridian height. The gun stood on a platform which was marked as a sundial, and therefore, simultaneously with the explosion, the gnomon cast its shadow on figure XII.[3]

As clocks came into fashion and technology advanced, the dial-makers were less in demand; it seemed as though they were destined to go the way of the muzzle-loading rifle. In 1872, Margaret Gatty, author of *The Book of Sundials*, wrote, "In spite, however, of the decay and destruction of older examples, the day of the sundial is not yet done. Many new ones have been set up within the last few years. Horizontal dials are still erected in gardens with their graceful pedestals, vertical ones on country houses, and occasionally on a school or public building." Today, 148 years later, there are original and impressive sundials that would have delighted Mrs. Gatty, as they are dramatic and noble installations located in city centers, on college campuses, in front of museums, and municipal parks.

The activities of the astrotourist should not be confined to what only happens at night, as the night is but a shadow cast by earth, giving us the darkness to see the stars. During the day, Sol shines too brightly for us to see other stars, but we can track the shadow cast by ingenious devices that not only tell the time of day but mark the solstices and equinoxes.

Some of these timekeepers go well beyond simple dials and venture into the realm of inspired and wondrous. In some countries, they are considered bona fide tourist attractions that would fall into the purse and the purveyor of astrotourism. Star clocks and sundials are an exemplary addition to any destination you create or manage. There is a wide assortment of dials that can be integrated, each with its own charm and characteristics.

- Horizontal dials
- Vertical dials
- Equatorial dials
- Polar dials
- Analemmatic dials
- Reflected ceiling dials
- Portable dials

The Sundial Bridge at Turtle Bay in Redding, California (1999 CE), has ultramodern elements, as it functions as both a cantilever bridge and a sundial. A towering edifice (66m) is located at one end, holding up the bridge and acting as the gnomon. The tower's shadow is cast upon a large dial to the north of the bridge, laid out on the ground; however, it is accurate only one day a year—the solstice. The tip of the shadow moves at approximately one foot per minute, providing the spectator the opportunity to meditate and reflect upon our spinning planet.[4]

Jantar Mantar (1724 CE), located in Delhi, India, is a popular destination with several various astronomical instruments, including the Samrat Yantra (Supreme Instrument), an equinoctial sundial of enormous proportions. It measures 90 feet high, and its shadow marks the

Figure 9.1 Sundial Bridge, Turtle Bay photo

Source: VisitRedding.com

time of day with extreme precision as it is capable of measuring time to an accuracy of two seconds. It remains one of the most popular tourist attractions in India. A small cupola on top is used for announcing eclipses and forecasting monsoons.[5]

One of the most visited places in the world is a sundial, the obelisk in Vatican City. This 25.5 m tall stone monolith acts as the gnomon for a sundial laid out on the pavement. This Egyptian obelisk was brought to Rome by Emperor Caligula in 37 AD and stood in its original spot, the Circus of Caligula, until 1586, when it was moved to the center of St. Peter's Square.[6] In 1817, the pavement of St. Peter's Square was inlaid with a compass rose and a sundial. The shadow cast marks the sun's movements at midday on the zodiac signs, and two inlaid discs act as markers for the winter and summer solstices.[7]

Astronomical Clocks

Another consideration for inclusion into the field of astrotourism is the astronomical clock. These highly visited landmarks hold all of the enchantment and whimsy of a toy maker's most eccentric contraption while being a precise technological device. When these mechanical curiosities began to appear in the 15th century, they were state-of-the-art; to this day, they command the attention of even the most jaundiced tourists. Along with telling the hour and minute of the day, these clocks correspond to the sun's movement as it passes through the zodiac, the planets, the phases of the moon, or the sky visible at a given time.[7]

Astronomical clocks are mostly found in city centers, and centuries later, they remain one of the most visited and highly rated attractions. The astro-tourist will see these landmarks with a nuanced and discerning eye, having a deeper understanding of what these clocks are measuring and tracking. They will inspire most every traveler, even as they carry a smartphone capable of extraordinary computing power. Though the Renaissance was still centuries away, astronomical clocks represented some of the most advanced technology of the day, spellbinding and mystifying the common man.

A sky as pure as water bathed the stars and brought them out.
—Antoine de Saint-Exupéry (poet/aviator)

Besançon, France (1860)

The Besançon Cathedral Clock is one of the world's most complex timepieces. The clock features 30,000 pieces, 70 dials, and 122 indicators. It tells the local time in 17 places around the world, times of sunrise and sunset, the time and height of the tides in eight French ports, has a perpetual calendar with leap year cycles, plus an orrery (mechanical model of the universe), and 21 automata. Clockmaker Auguste-Lucien Vérité constructed it, and over a century and a half later, it still is in working order. The clock is said to register up to 10,000 years (a claim that has yet to be proven), including adjustments for leap year cycles.[8]

Prague, Czech Republic (1410)

The Prague Orloj is the world's oldest working astronomical clock of its kind. It is located in the Old Town City Hall. A medieval clock that features an astronomical dial, "The Walk of the Apostles," features an hourly show of moving sculptures and a monthly calendar dial with the 12 signs of the zodiac. The clock is the center of Prague and it is still the city's most popular tourist attraction *six centuries later*.[9]

Lund, Sweden (1387)

This monumental timepiece, the Horologium Mirabile, contains exact and modern pieces of engineering. The Lund Cathedral was built in the mid-12th century, but the elegant astronomical clock was not installed until 1387. By calculating the moon's precise movements, this timepiece could determine the dates on which religious holidays would occur. The astronomical inner workings of the clock were updated to be accurate from 1923 to 2123.[10]

Figure 9.2 The Horologium Mirabile

Photo: Melissa Isla Venegas

Somerset, England, (circa 1386–1392)

The famous Wells Cathedral clock is considered to be the second oldest clock mechanism in Britain. The face is inside the church and displays the sun and moon's movements, the moon phases, and the time elapsed since the last new moon. It is crafted in the pre-Copernican model of the universe, where the earth is at the solar system center. Small automatons come to life on the quarter-hour, one of which (Jack Blandifer) strikes two bells with his hammers and heels. Concurrently, jousting knights appear above the clock face, while two striking jacks (in the form of knights in armor) appear on the outer face.[11]

Rouen, Normandy, France (1389)

The Gros-Horloge clockworks date from 1389, but the face and its current location date to the 16th century. The Renaissance facade is represented by a golden sun with 24 rays on a starry blue background. On the upper part of the dial, a recessed moon turns, revealing its phases; it completes a full rotation in 29 days. The weekdays are represented by Roman gods in an opening at the base of the dial.[12]

Figure 9.3 Zytglogge Tower Clock

Source: Copyright Bern Welcome

Bern, Switzerland (1530)

The Zytglogge tower holds a 15th-century astronomical clock that powers an hourly performance incorporating a dancing jester, parading bears, and a gilded figure, Chronos; he flips an hourglass and opens his mouth to swallow with each strike of the bell. The dial of the Zytglogge's astronomical clock is built in an astrolabe and has two faces, one on top of the other. It is divided into three zones: the black night sky, the deep blue zone of dawn, and the light blue day sky. A moon dial, displaying its phase, circles the zodiac's inner ring and features two suns. The smaller one indicates the date on the calendar dial, and the larger one circles the zodiac, with one revolution per year.[13]

Venice, Italy (1496–1499)

St. Mark's Clock on the Piazza San Marco displays the time, the moon phase, and the sun's current location in one of the 12 Zodiac signs. The clock tower is topped by two bronze figures that strike a bell hourly.[14] Twice a year, on the sixth of January (Epiphany) and the Thursday that occurs 40 days after Easter (Ascension Day), automatons behind the clock animate and make an appearance. Led by an angel with a trumpet, the three mechanical Magi pass before the Virgin and Child and disappear.[15]

Cremona, Italy (1583–1588)

The resplendent astronomical clock in the Torrazzo bell tower is the largest in the world and is a true masterpiece of engineering. The face is the sky, replete with zodiac constellations through which the sun and moon move. The hands denote the hours, the lunar phases, the months, the constellations, and the zodiac signs. Another hand completes a full circle every 18 years and three months (the Metonic cycle); when the sun and the moon hands are superimposed, it means that an eclipse is taking place.[16]

Lier, Belgium (1930)

The Zimmer tower was built in the 14th century, but the clockwork inside was made in the 20th century. The dial face consists of 12 different

Figure 9.4 Torrazo Bell Tower Clock

Image: @fotografarechepassione

clocks encircling a central one. The encircling clocks indicate time on all continents, phases of the moon, tidal movement, Metonic cycle, solar cycle, lunar cycle, and zodiac signs. Unlike any other astronomical clock, it tracks the earth's wobble process, which cycles over *25,800 years*; unsurprisingly, it holds the world's record for the slowest clock pointer. At each quarter-hour, automatons come to life that depicts three phases of life: child, adolescent, and adult; when the hour strikes, an old man appears, joining the other three. The noon hour (like most clocks) displays the biggest pageant, which consists of a celebratory parade of kings, mayors, and burgomasters from the last 100 years.[17]

CHAPTER 10

Tours

O, thou art fairer than the evening air clad in the beauty of a thousand stars.

—Christopher Marlowe (playwright)

Some locations are leveraging their attractions through building tours that create both context and content; connecting the dots creates a constellation of experiences from which a narrative is born. There is more to engage than just the sense of sight, even as astrotourism is primarily a visual activity. Not unlike a bottle of wine, which tells the people's story—what grapes are used, the terroir, and the history behind the vineyard, there is a unique story to every place. People who are enthusiasts seek out this information because it enriches the experience of wine drinking. It is the responsibility of an "astro-auteur" to define their presentation style to the guests they will be catering to.

The EU Star Route is an example of a tour created to emphasize the unique diversity of locations and contrasting cultures. Several European countries collaborated to promote astrotourism, or what they refer to as Star Tourism. This alliance established a route that traverses five countries and leads the astrotourist to particular locations to savor the stars and learn of the night sky's distinctive cultural interpretations. It is an all-encompassing spectrum of adventures, as the tour guides the traveler to the biggest solar observatory in the world and remote natural settings. Following are highlights of EU Star Route[1]

1. Tenerife, Spain: Volcano and Stars
   This distinctive isle has volcanoes and Spain's highest peaks. The "Summits of Tenerife" were accredited by the Starlight Foundation as a dark sky destination. There is access to professional stargazing equipment showcased at the world's biggest solar observatory, the Canaries Institute of Astrophysics (est. 1975), where visitors can see

the Museum of Science and the Cosmos. Nineteen countries have involvement, as the peaks of the Teide make the most of the area's ideal atmospheric conditions, which provide optimum stargazing.

2. Valencia, Spain: Inland and Rural

    Rural and inland tourism has seen a remarkable increase due to its dark skies. It is one of the region's most celebrated resources. A feature that stands out is the path of astrotourism between the towns of Alpuente and Aras de Los Olmos, where an observatory is located. The latter has the infrastructure, services, and activities to optimize the dark and clear night skies. There is "astrohiking," which combines star gazing and the scenery's grandeur while walking to the astronomical center of the Alto Turia, a UNESCO-designated Biosphere Reserve. These are defined as "learning places for sustainable development" and where local solutions are implemented to address global challenges.

3. Sardinia, Italy: Stones, Stars, and Paths

    This destination has a striking contrast between the ancient and state-of-the-art. There are guided tours for the internationally acclaimed Sardinia Radio Telescope and the Pranu Mutteddu, an ancient site with prehistoric standing stones (menhirs) with anthropomorphic shapes. A number of these menhirs are lined up from east to west, suggesting the probability that early man was tracking the sun's path. Also nearby is the Barumini, an exceptional bronze age archaeological ruin and UNESCO World Heritage Site. One of the other attractions for an astrotourist is the planetarium and museum of astronomy developed by the National Institute for Astrophysics and the Astronomical Observatory of Caligari.

4. Bieszczady Mountains, Poland: Nature and Sky

    This stop along the Star Route showcases the deep forests of the Eastern Carpathian Mountains, far away from any human-made lights. The skies are a draw for those who seek out a pristine night in a natural setting. It has a Starry-Sky preserve designation and is on the UNESCO World Cultural and Heritage List.

5. Taxiarchis, Greece: Myths and Astronomy

    This tour begins in Thessaloniki, home to the Science Centre and Technology Museum, *Noesis*. An installation presents the constellations and their myths in exhibits that include a digital planetarium,

3D simulator, 3D IMAX cinema, technology museum, and a permanent exhibition about ancient Greek technology. The tour includes ascending to Taxiarchis, a traditional mountain village located on Mount Holomontas (altitude 670 meters), for a night of stargazing.

An astrotourism destination will not necessarily come into existence due to the presence of an observatory; however, the latter is a determinant of a prerequisite condition—a quality dark sky. Connecting with people under a night sky with inexpensive equipment (or none at all), combined with a good knowledge of the stars and their stories, can deliver a rewarding and memorable evening. The stories are there, the pictures are there, and it is up to the astropreneur to put the pieces together for the guests.

6. EU Star Route Report—Bulgaria

There are no certified dark sky areas in Bulgaria, and activities are concentrated in observatories and planetaria. There are six observatories positioned in Bulgaria's larger cities, the largest of which is the NAO Rozhen on Rhodopa mountain. Though many smaller towns have a planetarium, the most well equipped and notable is in Smolyan. Telescopes are available for viewing at the astronomical observatories, but there are no stargazing workshops for tourists.[2]

Chilean Tours

The Atacama Desert, located high in the Andean mountain range, possesses climatological and geographic characteristics that create a unique environment. As mentioned earlier, an indicator of the quality of the skies is the number of observatories erected. In the last decades, Chile has become a leading country in the field of astronomy. It has the most developed astrotourism industry globally, with 21.3 percent of international tourists claiming that their overarching motivation to travel to Chile was for the dark skies and astronomical pursuits. Due to its southern sky exposure, one can observe, among other things, the center of the Milky Way and the Magellanic Clouds. To service this new market, agencies that offer stargazing trips with sophisticated and upscale optical equipment have opened for business in the municipalities of Santiago, La Serena, San Pedro de Atacama, Antofagasta, and Iquique.[3]

Unlike tourist observatories, which can be visited at night to make observations through telescopes on site, the observatories staffed by scientists are open to the public only during daytime hours. Tours can be booked to view the facilities and learn about the telescopes and what goes on in the control rooms; however, they may *not* make observations through the equipment.

In 2015 the Chilean president, Michelle Bachelet, said, "It is estimated that by the year 2020, 70% of global astronomical infrastructure will be concentrated in our country, with the most powerful telescopes ever installed, and an investment close to $6 billion."[4] At this writing, there are 12 observatories in Chile, with plans for four more.

Telescope viewing is available for visitors at these listed observatories.[5]

Mamalluca Observatory was constructed at an altitude of 1,200 m, becoming the first tourist observatory in Chile. Located near the city of Vicuña, Mamalluca, offers an astronomical program tailored for the general public that consists of a lecture, along with celestial viewing using a medium-sized and a larger principal telescope. Also, there is a diner and souvenir shop located on-site. The tour lasts four hours.

Collowara Observatory is perched on Mt. Cerro Churqui at an altitude of 1,300 m and is one of the newest tourist observation facilities situated near the town of Andacollo. The main observation dome houses a 14-inch Cassigrain Smith telescope ($5,000–$7,000), and there are terraces with two automatic 10-inch Smith Newtonian ($650–$825) telescopes, as well as a 16-inch Dobsonian telescope ($2,000–$3,000 range). Atacama Desert dark sky clarity (Priceless). The tour is about two hours.

Pangue Observatory is situated in a mountainous landscape at 1,478 m, close to the Elqui Valley, and near the little town of Vicuña. It is next to the Tololo, Soar, and Gemini observatories. It offers 25-inch, 16-inch, and 12-inch telescopes with guides who speak Spanish, English, and French. Their standard tours are two hours; however, you can lease the facility by the evening for customized events.

Cruz del Sur Observatory is located at an altitude of 1,100 m on the Combarbalá plain south of the town of La Serena. It consists of four domes, each equipped with 14-inch and 16-inch digital telescopes. The facility was opened in 2009 to boost astronomical tourism in the Andean countryside. This auspicious endeavor changed the city, and it became one of the leading astronomy education centers in the Coquimbo area.

Paniri Caur Observatory is located at an altitude of 2,525 m in the town of Chiu-Chiu. It markets a tour, which includes an audiovisual lecture, observation of classical and indigenous constellations using star charts, a 14-inch telescope, and a planetarium show. The duration of the tour is about three hours.

ALMA Observatory (The Atacama Large Millimeter Array) is akin to the Very Large Array (VLA) in New Mexico, where the movie *Contact* was filmed. ALMA is a cluster of 66 radio-telescopic antennas situated at an altitude of 5,058 m on the de Chajnantor Plain in the Andes Mountain Range.[6] It required a global collaboration to create this one-of-a-kind observatory, which was the first to capture an image of a black hole.[7] Its extreme altitude requires a parka, gloves, a hat with ear protection, and wind pants; sunglasses and sunburn protection are encouraged. Altitude sickness is a real concern at this height, and people may experience headache, dizziness, nausea, or rapid heartbeat; they *must* pass a physical examination to visit.

A correlation may be established between the development of international observatories in Chile and South Africa, where the South African Large Telescope is located, and the growth of local astrotourism. Like planets falling into orbit around a star, local commercial enterprises have launched near and around the observatory. As it relates to observatories and astronomy, the economic emergence occurring in Chile and South Africa may be compared to what occurred in Scotland in 1947.

At the first Edinburgh International Festival, classical performers of music, theatre, opera, and dance were invited from around the world. Eight uninvited local theater groups showed up, calling themselves "Festival Adjuncts," but the term "Fringe Festival" stuck instead. Eventually, the Fringe grew larger than the original festival, and the concept spread globally. Today, 73 years later, there are 250 Fringe Festivals around the world.

It is plausible that local dark sky economies and astropreneurs will surpass revenues created by the original scientific establishments, create more jobs, and spread to other places across the planet without requiring a costly anchor, such as a multi-million-dollar observatory. The same knowledge necessary to create and run a dark sky destination is not site-specific, and the same tools will be applicable in Africa, Australia, Asia, the Americas, and Europe—anywhere darkness rules the night.

Sundial Trails

Numerous locations worldwide have sundial tours, and some cities have walking trails that provide the participant with maps to hunt down these shadowy monuments that are an homage to our nearest star. Sundials are known to be etched with short, pithy mottos, which are part of their enduring charm. They remind us of the impermanence of life, and these axioms should be in Latin, a dead language:

Omnes vulnerant, ultima necat
All [hours] wound, the last one kills

The Hautes-Alpes region has a total area of 5,549 km², boasts over 400 sundials, and is home to the largest number of painted sundials in France. Multiple trails meander through the region, with one circuit that takes the traveler through the locales of the Queyras Valley, Briançonnais, Vallouise, and the Embrunais. The city of Briançon alone has 18 dials with an ancestral tradition that dates from the 18th century. This living heritage is preserved, with contemporary models being fashioned to this day. These magnificent star-tethered instruments decorate the façades of numerous monuments, public buildings, villages, and townhouses. Some dials are simple and modest that feature maxims and religious sayings, while others are elaborate works of art fashioned as frescoes or sculptures.

On the Route des Cadrans Solaires, the traveler will find the Castillon Dam, the world's largest sundial—95 meters high and 200 meters wide. The dam was built in 1948, but the sundial was inaugurated in 2009 to attract tourists. Rather than the typical gnomon, the dam's face is etched with lines that mark the hours.[8]

Lente hora, celeriter anni
An hour passes slowly, but the years go by quickly.

Besançon, France

There are 10 exceptional sundials in the historical center of Besançon. Walking this trail takes approximately 60 to 90 minutes. The dial on the chapel at Lycée Pasteur is unique, as along with telling the time of day, it marks the solstices and equinoxes. It is etched with the Latin inscription that translates to, "While the sun shines, I speak; without the sun, I am quiet."[9]

Paris, France

Cadrans Solaires de Paris (Sundials of Paris) is a book with an inventory of more than 100 of the city's sundials. The earliest sundials are on churches, where they have long aided travelers to know the time of prayers. The sundials themselves are fascinating, and many are inscribed with such apt reflections on the nature of time that they are worth seeking out for those snippets of truth alone.[10] Walking the trail becomes a treasure hunt for sententious *bon mots* inspired by our neighborhood star's light and shadow play.

Les heures fuient; La justice reste
The hours flee; justice stays.

In Houston, Texas, there is a one-day excursion that includes seven unusual public sundials that have been adopted into the hearts and minds of the city's residents. The 99 km long tour takes approximately five hours to complete by automobile. Additional side trips to another seven dials are also available.[11] In a city awash with ALAN, the astrotourist has, in at least one way, an opportunity to commune with a star by visiting these silent sentinels to the sun.

In Seattle, Washington, there are 20 sundials, the oldest of which was built in 1909; the latest was installed in 2006. Each dial is distinctive in its style, type, materials used, and artistic interpretation, departing from the mundane horizontal version that uses a skyward aimed gnomon. The route requires transport by car but is possible to circumnavigate by fit cyclists. The total distance is 27 km and may take anywhere from four to 10 hours to complete.[12]

London, England

London's most informative sundial is near Tower Hill's tube station. It stands as a landmark as it tells the history of London and the London transport. In AD 43, using carved illustrations to tell the story, it traces time from when the city was Londinium (its Roman name) up to the Thames Barrier building between 1975 and 1982. London's greatest selection of sundials can be found in the Horniman Gardens at Forest Hill, where 11 different types of dials have been assembled over the last 25 years.[13] Over thousands of years, countries and cultures used sundials to establish daily and seasonal routines by measuring the closest star's movement. While sundials epigrams may have inspired us to contemplate our mortality, it is upon a starry night where we ponder eternity.

Night Sky Tour

The Messier Marathon goal is to view 110 deep space objects over one evening and an excellent objective for the ardent stellar aficionado. These objects were discovered by the French astronomer Charles Messier (1730–1817), who was looking for comets and stumbled upon these significant celestial objects. This epic jaunt around the universe involves viewing nebulae, globular clusters, open clusters, and distant galaxies, making it extremely popular for amateur astronomers possessing all levels of experience and equipment. The best viewing windows are moonless nights in the spring or fall. A telescope with an 8-inch aperture is necessary to view galaxies beyond our own, and they range from $400 to over $2,000.[14]

CHAPTER 11

ALAN and Health

There is stardust in your veins. We are literally, ultimately, children of the stars.

—Jocelyn Bell Burnell (astrophysicist)

This chapter will cover ALAN's impact on nocturnal life, human health, the environment, and how anthropogenic activities were an impetus for astrotourism. To comprehensively serve the astrotourist, the operator must show the exigencies of the light pollution crises. Astrotourism becomes a framework to convey information on the societal impact of ALAN.

A tourist who travels to Provence, France, for cooking classes brings home more than the memory of cooking and eating a meal; they bring home knowledge. Just as the chef may impart the philosophy and practice behind "farm to table" and the need to perpetuate sustainable agricultural practices to the guest, so too can the astrotour operator impart ALAN's overarching issues and what can be done to preserve dark skies.

Our earliest known ancestor is *Graecopithecus freybergi*, a hominid that lived 7.2 million years ago.[1] Our cellular makeup evolved from our interconnection and exposure to the sun, moon, stars, and fire. For at least a million years, man has had control of fire.[2] With only the agreement of a few astronomers and an ophthalmologist, my assertion is the human eye evolved due to the influence of these light sources. The cells in our eyes would have shaped themselves to adapt to firelight, which glows between 1700 K and 1850 K (K= Kelvin). The kelvin is the base unit of temperature in the International System of Units[3] and is a useful measurement to understand when the time comes to choose the light for a dark sky destination.

Fire's warm glow is pleasing and comfortable to the human eye, as candles do something to us psychologically; otherwise, it would not be considered "romantic lighting." Gazing into fire does not affect the eyes the same way as staring at the moon, which glows at 4000 K. Firelight does not cause the pupil to constrict, which would impede one's vision at night. A wide-open pupil allows more photons to hit the retina, essential for night vision, a critical attribute to survive nocturnal predators. It stands to reason that our eyes and optic nerve adapted to the warm glow of firelight over millennia.

The world's history changed in 1882 when the Pearl Street power station powered up and began generating electricity for about 400 lamps. Within two years after Pearl Street came online, the station was serving 508 customers with 10,164 lamps![4] That number has always increased and continues to grow with no sign of abating.

In only 137 years or 0.0019027777777777775 percent of human history, our technology altered the nighttime biospheres across the planet. The natural rhythm of day and night has been permanently transformed, and scientists only became aware of the consequences a few decades ago. Electrical lights have plundered the darkness of the night and created a "false day."

Circadian rhythms are physical, mental, and behavioral changes that follow a daily cycle that responds primarily to light and darkness in an organism's environment. Sleeping at night and being awake during the day is an example. The main cue influencing circadian rhythms is daylight. Circadian rhythms are found in most living things, including animals, plants, and even microbes. Irregular rhythms have been linked to various chronic health conditions, such as sleep disorders, obesity, diabetes, depression, bipolar disorder, and seasonal affective disorder.[5]

In 2016 one of the sessions at the National Toxicology Program, put on by the U.S. Department of Health and Human Services, listed their workshop this way:

"Shift Work at Night, Artificial Light at Night, and Circadian Disruption" Many people experience interruptions in light-dark cycles due to their lifestyle choices (e.g., use of electronic devices at night), location of their residences (e.g., urban light pollution), or working at night (e.g., shift work). Exposures to artificial light at night (ALAN) or changes in the timing of exposures to natural light (such as with "jet lag") may disrupt biological processes controlled by endogenous circadian rhythms, potentially resulting in adverse health outcomes.[6]

The French Agency for Food, Environmental and Occupational Health and Safety (ANSES) warned that exposure to intense and powerful LED light is "photo-toxic." [It] can cause an irreversible loss of retinal cells and lead to a common cause of blindness. Regardless of the ecosystem studied, scientific knowledge has convergingly shown an increase in mortality and decreased the diversity of animal and plant species studied in environments illuminated at night, including by LED lighting.[7]

Experiencing the night sky provides perspective, inspiration and leads us to reflect on our humanity and place in the universe.[8] Perhaps future studies will produce empirical evidence that proves an erosion of the human psyche when the starlight is no longer a part of our mortal diet. As spas are frequented to refresh and rejuvenate our minds and bodies, would similar results be achieved from a dark sky vacation rejuvenating the eyes and souls?

Dacher Keltner, a psychologist at the University of California, Berkeley, points out that the star-splashed canvas rotating overhead elicits a sense of wonder and awe that may translate into positive human behaviors. In laboratory studies, participants who had recently encountered that experience scored higher on assessments of scientific reasoning and were kinder, more altruistic, and less materialistic.[9]

The electric light, using an incandescent, began delivering illumination at 2400K. Today LED headlights on automobiles illuminate the road ahead of the driver with 6000K, and many people find these new lights to be blinding. There are numerous online groups (Ban Blinding LEDs) and petitions circulating to ban LED headlights.[10] "Many people who find it difficult to focus at night or find the glare from oncoming headlights and traffic lights debilitating often suffer from astigmatism, where the eye's curvature distorts light."[11]

The student of this topic will be well served to understand that its impact can only be mitigated through a concerted effort by a large population segment due to ALAN's ubiquitous nature. Though no empirical studies have been conducted, it is my best assertion that light pollution, star-starved cities, and electrical lighting impact are linked to the yearning to seek out darkness and an astrotourism experience.

The detrimental effects of high-intensity LED lighting are not limited to humans. Excessive outdoor lighting disrupts many species that need a dark environment. For instance, poorly designed LED lighting disorients some birds, insects, turtle, fish species, and U.S. national parks have adopted optimal lighting designs and practices that minimize light pollution's effects on the environment.[12]

ALAN can have a debilitating effect on trees and other vegetation. "Artificial lighting, especially from a source that emits in the red to the infrared range of the spectrum, extends the day length and can change flowering patterns, and most importantly, promote continued growth long after it is safe for the trees to do so, due to a coming winter."[13]

The scientific and medical community created guidelines that instruct which specific frequencies on the electromagnetic spectrum can be harmful. We know that too much time under the sun will burn your flesh and cause cancers due to exposure to ultraviolet radiation. We know that too many x-rays can increase the likelihood of cancer. Gamma rays from nuclear sources and radioactive materials are deadly. We now understand the environmental impact and health hazards with the light on the visible spectrum. The impact of light can vary from species to species and wavelength to wavelength.

Human health is also adversely affected by light pollution as light during night time hours has been linked to human cancers and psychological disorders.[12] Many birds migrate at night and navigate by the moon and star reflections. Excessive nighttime lighting can lead to reflections on glass high-rise towers and other objects, causing confusion, collisions, and the death of millions of birds each year. A Canadian group raised this issue in 1993, and by 1999 the Audubon Society and partners started a movement that currently has 33 cities in the United States, which extinguishes their ALAN during bird migrations.[14] Participation in and promotion of astrotourism will have a beneficial collateral influence on the environment.

CHAPTER 12

Sharing the Stars With Your Guests

*That is the exploration that awaits you! Not mapping stars and study-
ing nebula, however, charting the unknown possibilities of existence.*

—Leonard Nimoy (actor)

The oldest stories ever told are those of the stars. We ceaselessly witnessed them throughout our tenure on planet Earth. Without fail, the stars made their grand entrance from the east, rising to the night sky's zenith, then plunged into the western horizon. While they were aloft, we ruminated about their meaning and created our own. The quest of the astrotourist is both the exploration of the night sky and how the night sky has shaped the history of humanity.

A good place to begin is educating your guest on twilight and its three phases, civil, nautical, and astronomical twilight.

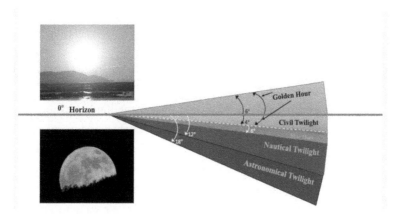

Figure 12.1 Golden Hour/Twilight Distinctions

Source: Image by Author

Civil Twilight

When the sun's geometric center is 6 degrees below the horizon marks the threshold of civil twilight. In the morning, it begins at 6 degrees below and ends when the sun crests the horizon. In the evening, it starts at sunset and ends at 6 degrees beneath the horizon. Absent of fog or other atmospheric impediments, the brightest stars and planets can be seen as well as objects on the horizon or around you. Artificial lighting is unnecessary.

Nautical Twilight

When the sun's geometric center is 12 degrees below the horizon marks the threshold of nautical twilight. The term originates with sailors still able to take reliable readings via prominent stars as the horizon is still visible even without the moon's illumination. The outline of a terrestrial object will be discernable, with no atmospheric restrictions, but one's detailed outdoor activities have limits without the use of artificial illumination.

Astronomical Twilight

When the sun's geometric center is 18 degrees below the horizon marks the threshold of astronomical twilight. At this point, most casual observers would regard the night a wholly dark and particularly in an urban or suburban setting where light pollution is prevalent. The horizon is not discernable, and fainter stars and planets are visible with the naked eye. For a completely dark sky, the sun needs to be more than 18 degrees below the horizon to allow for the observation of galaxies, nebula, and other deep space objects.

Identifying one's first constellation provokes the kind of exuberance we see in children who learn their first words; a new world opens up. It is a first step toward acquiring their "space legs" to navigate the celestial firmament that dutifully appears every evening. We have always looked to the stars to see what they portend and conceived adages as, "It is in the stars," "star-crossed lovers," or "my lucky star," or want to know if one's "star is rising." The first star-sign astrology column began in 1930 and has captivated the attention of millions of readers across our planet.[1] Astrotourists look for meaning in the tapestry of the night sky because it connects them to the universe. How is it possible to resist experiencing a convergence with the cosmic when infinity is spinning overhead? The stars have been a source of inspiration throughout time, and though much of it has been lost due to our urban lifestyles, it is being reawakened through astrotourism.

With the stars as a constant, we learned to navigate land and sea, giving us the means to spread our species. By studying the stars, the ancients knew how to foretell the seasons, animal movements, and civilizations sprung up. For some cultures, the stars informed them when the rains would come when it was time to shear the sheep, and in the case of Australia's aboriginals when it was time to collect the emu eggs.

Cultures throughout time, bound by their relationship to the night sky, created their own unique stories. We experience the rotation of the earth, as the stars crest over the horizon, as it spins at speeds that would belie the gentle ride we experience. The earth's surface at the equator moves at a speed of 460 meters per second—or roughly 1,000 miles per hour.[2] As the constellations emerge from the darkness of the horizon, they bring with them the legends and myths that have endured throughout the ages.

In the early 1920s, the International Astronomical Union (IAU) decided upon 88 constellations officially recognized by all astronomers. The breakdown consists of 17 human or mythological characters, 29 inanimate objects, and 42 animals. Stories about the constellations are told worldwide, in a myriad of languages and by many cultures. The Greco-Roman astronomer Ptolemy named 48 of the 88 constellations we know today, with many already considered constellations by his forebears, like Leo the Lion. This constellation was one of the earliest names, and in one Leo myth, the lion and Hercules do battle. The marauding Nemean lion terrorized the countryside yet had a hide so tough it could not be harmed by any weapon known to man, leaving our hero to fight the beast with his bare hands.

No matter where your travels take you or accommodate the astrotourist, the constellations are overheard with a completely different palette of stars in the southern hemisphere. The northern array was full of narratives from ancient civilizations, with some dating back 6,000 years ago. Historians have concluded that the Greek constellations originated in the Mesopotamian civilizations of the ancient Babylonians and Sumerians. Their stories, legends, and myths are full of monsters, heroes, villains,

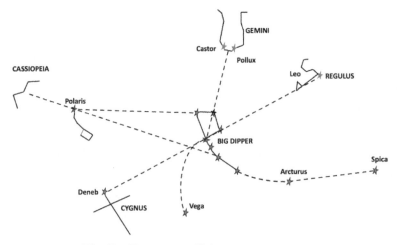

Figure 12.2 The Big Dipper as a Pointer

Source: Image created by Author

treachery, comedy, tragedy, and drama. To remember these nighttime narratives, constellations and asterisms became illustrations and mnemonics of the sky. An example is using the Big Dipper to locate other constellations in the sky and the prominent stars within each.

Story telling predated the written word and was shared to educate, entertain, instill values and morals, and preserve cultural identities. Stories are universal as they can bridge cultural, linguistic, and age-related divides. Stories are effective educational tools because listeners become engaged and therefore remember. Storytelling can be seen as a foundation for learning and teaching.[3]

Astrotourism is a global attraction and not based on a specific cultural underpinning. To see Angkor Wat, one has to travel to Cambodia and explore Amsterdam's canals; one has to travel to the Netherlands. Traveling to a country is to experience their social and ethnic identities, and it is expressed through their folklore, art, architecture, and food. These accomplishments are an outgrowth of the country's people, essence, and identity, but the stars' stories predate modern civilizations by the millennium. Long before civilizations grew to become the countries we know today, people told stories about stars laid down by the ancients.

From 1989 to 2018, my company toured a theatrical production created to raise awareness of our night sky's loss due to light pollution. There was an engagement in Rome, and upon entering the theater, the question was posed, "How old?" The house manager responded, "900." Startled by the response, "This place is 900 years old!?" He answered, "No, it was built in 900." "900 AD! This place is ancient!" To which the curator said, "No, in Rome, that is just old."

Even in a city that can easily trace its history back 2,500 years, it is still a blink-of-an-eye on the clock representing our time on earth. Human's connection with the stars began before language, writing, architecture, or pottery shards. Western civilization perpetuated the star myths of ancient Greece and those narratives are the ones we are most familiar with. They are far from the whole picture; like the night sky, we will never see all of it at once and the range is stellar.

The Lummi Tribe of the Pacific Northwest tells how Coyote liked to take out his eyeballs and juggle them to impress the girls. One day, while juggling, he threw one so high it stuck in the sky and became the star, Aldebaran. In Hawai'i, the demi-god Maui used his "Manaiakalani," a magical fish hook (the tail of Scorpio) and with it caught the ocean floor. He thought he had an enormous fish on the line and reeled up the bottom of the ocean to the surface. His catch became the mountains of the new islands, resulting in the birth of Polynesia.

Though Western civilization's constellations in the Northern Hemisphere were named after Greek myths, the planets were named after Roman gods, and Arabic cultures named the stars. For Western astronomy, most of the accepted star names are Arabic, a few are Greek, and some are of unknown origin. Typically, only bright stars have names.[4] Many of the prominent stars known today are of Arabic origin as they bear names given to them during the golden age of Islamic astronomy (9th–13th centuries). The majority of stars' names are related to their constellation, for example, the star Deneb means "tail" and labels that part of Cygnus the Swan. Others describe the star itself, such as Sirius, which translates literally as "scorching," aptly named as it is the brightest star in the sky. Many prominent stars bear Arabic names, in which "al" corresponds to the article "the" and often appears in front, for example, Algol, "The Ghoul" (10th century).[5]

The intent here is to ignite the reader's enthusiasm and imagination and gird them to familiarize themselves with the many tales of the night sky as it will become the content for your guest's evenings under the stars.

They have enthralled people for thousands of years and will stimulate the curiosity and entertain today's astrotourist. There are numerous books on the subject, with some listed in the Resources.

The following story shows how various cultures over millennia used one star. Alpha Ceti is the Bayer classification for a star in the Southern Hemisphere. The Bayer classification was created by the astronomer Johann Bayer in 1603, who circulated a system identifying all the stars visible to the naked eye.[6] More than a thousand years before Johann named it, it was called Menkar, or in Arabic, Al-Minkhar meaning "nostril," and it is the part of the constellation Cetus, the sea monster. Perseus had to slay the monster to save Andromeda (also the name of a galaxy) and the other chief characters in the Perseus legend, Cepheus, Cassiopeia as well Andromeda, Cetus, and Perseus, all have their place in the night sky as constellations.[7] The term cetacean derives from Cetus, which in Latin literally means, "huge fish."

Three and half centuries later, the Star Trek franchise made reference to the same star Bayer name, in a 1967 episode "Space Seed," and in the 1987 movie "Star Trek II: The Wrath of Khan" but reversed Bayer's designation to "Ceti Alpha V." The reason this is mentioned is that it was one of the most iconic episodes in people's memory of the Star Trek franchise and demonstrates the durability of star lore.

Given that most people, especially the adventure traveler and outdoor enthusiast, love whales and dolphins (there is constellation Delphinus, the Dolphin), they will be delighted to learn this interesting anecdote. Interestingly, Greek mythology gods did not place themselves into the night skies but were responsible for placing mortals into the heavens to memorialize their deeds, their treachery, heroism, and impart upon the generations to follow what it meant to live a stellar life. The references to the stars are with us still and will always continue to be written into our own stories and legends.

Millennials are fast becoming increasingly sophisticated travelers, less destination-oriented and more (authentic) experience-oriented. From Antarctica to remote parts of Newfoundland, it is the unique experience tourists seek and are sharing through social media. The search for eclectic adventures takes travelers of all ages to winter locations, no longer put off by the cold or even a barren winter landscape.[8] A pristine nightscape, replete with the constellation's mythological stories, makes their entrance from the east and their exit to the west. It is a unique and wondrous adventure that appeals to both today's and tomorrow's adventure traveler.

Australia has vast stretches of "Outback" that makes up about 6 million acres, bigger than several European countries.[9] Australian Aboriginals can claim to be the oldest continuous living culture on the planet. Recent dating of the earliest known archaeological sites on the Australian continent—using thermo-luminescence and other modern dating techniques—have pushed back the date for aboriginal presence in Australia to at least 40,000 years. Some of the evidence points to dates over 60,000 years old.[10] As old as the stories are about the constellations laid down by ancient Greece, compared to Australia's aboriginal culture, they are embryonic in comparison. In Australia, one of the best-known Aboriginal constellations is the Emu. It is an exquisite spectacle that is more convincing and apparent than European constellations. In Ku-Ring-Gai Chase National Park is a rock engraving of an emu, and when the Emu in the Sky stands above her portrait, in the correct orientation, it is when real-life emus are laying their eggs.[11]

While most people easily identify Orion's belt, their knowledge of who he was or how he got into the night sky is a mystery waiting to be revealed. This is just a single tale from one civilization at one point in time in the planet's history. There are many legends and myths from various dormant cultures waiting to be shared again. As the tales of the stars come to life, they will give the astrotourist a rich, informative, memorable, and insightful experience as they learn about the constellations. They yearn for the relatable and subjects that broaden their horizon. Just as the "star-tales" of ancient Greece were a popular form of make-believe, our broad-based love of science fiction/fantasy is a way to connect travelers with the night sky overhead and spark their musings with what once was and what could still be.

The well-known constellations, begun by the Sumerians and adopted by the Greeks, was limited by what could be seen in the Northern Hemisphere. It was not until the 16th century, almost two thousand years later, when European explorers traveled south of the equator and were exposed to a categorically different night. For one, the constant of a North Star was gone; it would have been a wonderment for the sailors to see a night sky so contrary and polar to anything they knew, not unlike the first time astrotourist today. These new sightings and findings were grouped into

Figure 12.3 Emu in the sky (photo credit Barnaby Norris)

new sets of constellations named after the new species they encountered, like Pavo the Peacock.

Here, a moment is taken to set some history straight. Johannes Bayer was accredited to the 12 new constellations included in his publication Uranometria in 1603[6]. However, he made the star charts based upon the sailors' discovery and navigators who made the journey years earlier. The First Dutch Expedition to Nusantara (Indonesia) was a sailing trip from 1595 to 1597. The navigator Peter Dirkszoon Keyser and some colleagues on the first Dutch trading expedition to the East Indies, known as the Eerste Schip Vaart[12] (First Shipping). The observations made on the Eerste Schip Vaart had gone directly to the Dutch cartographer Petrus Plancius in Amsterdam. These stars, divided into the 12 new southern constellations, first appeared on a globe produced jointly by him and Jodocus Hondius in 1598. Hondius published revised versions of this globe in 1600 and 1601.[13] The Dutch historian Elly Dekker has demonstrated that Bayer almost certainly copied the southern stars' positions from these Hondius globes, as he had no original observations to work from.[12]

Between 1751 and 1754, the French astronomer Nicolas-Louis de Lacaille was stationed at the Cape of Good Hope and cataloged the positions of 9,766 southern stars in just 11 months. Unlike many of the larger, brighter constellations, which were chiefly based on mythology and legend, Lacaille chose to fill uncharted areas of the southern sky with new constellations representing inanimate objects—apparently a personal resolution he made to honor artisans by their tools and inventions. He is considered "the Columbus of the starry southern skies." [14]

From the perspective of European astronomers and explorers, who put their stamp on the Southern Hemisphere's night sky by naming groupings of stars into constellations, there were no legends or myths associated with them. Perhaps, because at this point civilization was living in the "Age of Reason" that began with Descartes and Newton, there was no space in space for fanciful myths and extraordinary stories to entertain and educate. "It looks like somebody's attic!" was how Heber D. Curtis, director of the Allegheny Observatory, described Lacaille's chart of constellations. Consider leaving it to your guests to fill in the back story of how the Pendulum Clock, the Artist's Easel, or the Sculptor's Chisel found their way into the night sky.

There is an endless number of night tales as told by the Navajo, Shoshone, Pueblo, Hopi, Zuni, Apache, Zulu, Tswana, Xhosa, Bedouin, Maoris, Innuit, Incans, Mayan, Aztecs, Chinese, Hindu, and the Bushman. Every place an astrotourist travels to, there is a lore to be re-told anew and will be illustrated by the stars that sweep overhead every evening.

CHAPTER 13

Developing a Destination

We are all in the gutter, but some of us are looking at the stars.

—Oscar Wilde (poet/playwright)

This chapter is a DIY lesson and a "how to" base on case studies from other locations and the author's recommendations. Because astrotourism is an adventure into the unknown on both earth and in the sky, there is latitude for the enterprising purveyor in this field. Considering that astrotourism was once limited to astronomers, which is a new field of tourism for most of the population, innovative ideas and creativity will be indispensable in developing a destination. It is up to the entrepreneur to create the newcomer's context as there are far more of those individuals than astronomers.

This kind of tourism elicits a tremendous amount of sharing and camaraderie. People with telescopes are eager to share the view. It is impossible to overconsume a night sky, and there is always more than enough for everybody. Unlike a beach, a resort, or parks where there are only so many choice parking places and spots by the shore, a night sky is vast and cannot be used up, nor is one place under the sky better than another (skyglow and light pollution excluded). No matter how much one learns to pass on to their guests, there will be other guests who will further your knowledge of astronomy, sharing their skills, wisdom, and enthusiasm.

It (astrotourism) can draw many visitors to a destination where skies are free from artificial light pollution. These desolate places with their apparent emptiness, once disregarded by earlier travelers, have now become noteworthy attractions.[1]

The attraction, a dark sky, is already in place without any capital outlay. There are no user fees, royalties, or residuals that need to be paid. It never breaks down, the lease will never run out, and there can be no copyright infringement as the content, and the stories were written thousands of years ago. It requires no maintenance and no upkeep; however, it does require protection. There is tremendous latitude in constructing a location or not creating anything and leaving it empty.

As people will be traveling hundreds, if not thousands of miles, to access a pristine night sky, they will require overnight accommodations. Star viewers may stay up all hours of the night and, therefore, more likely to be sleeping later into the morning. People who require sleeping arrangements will find blackout curtains very welcome. Sleep masks could be offered up in place of curtains with your own logo printed on them as a take-home gift and memento of your guests' stay.

As such, astrotourism provides opportunities for unexpected collaborations between the tourism stakeholders, local communities, and scientific institutions.[2] Getting the participation of stakeholders is critical to the success of a dark sky destination. Communities near dark zones may continue to increase tourism and their growth if the outdoor lighting is properly designed to protect the stars' view. Current common lighting practices in most municipalities are the anathema of the dark skies people are coming to see.

A growing number of locations worldwide are acquiring an International Dark-Sky Association (IDA) dark sky or Starlight Foundation certification which entails broad participation by the community as the outdoor lighting needs of government, business, and residents are not uniform.

The development of a dark sky asset will require the locale to rethink their nighttime lighting. A dark sky has particular needs to be restored, preserved, and protected but is inexpensive to implement compared to the restoration of other natural resources (i.e., rivers, lakes, watersheds). Community illumination may require recalibrating as an improper design can reduce starlight's visibility with an overabundance of outdoor lighting, which will diminish the quality of a starry sky.

Overcoming people's reflexive fear of the dark and their paradigm for what it means to be safe has been a major obstacle. Decision making is not logical; it is emotional, according to the latest findings in neuroscience.[3] As a rule, people think that more light means more safety, but research shows this not the case. A study led by the London School of Hygiene and Tropical Medicine in partnership with the University College of London found no evidence of a link between reduced street lighting and nighttime collisions or increased crime.[4] No solid evidence has

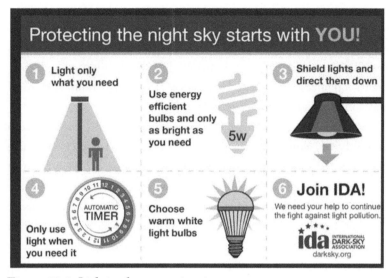

Figure 13.1 Lighting best practices image

Source: International Dark Sky Association

yet been found to support the hypothesis that improved street lighting reduces reported crime.[5] Studies were conducted to find some correlation between nighttime lighting and crime in major metropolitan areas. Any municipality near a dark sky destination will be considerably smaller and not have the same crime metrics. However, people's superstitions about the dark endure regardless of the population density of their community.

If you are a stakeholder in a community near dark skies, it is in your interest to adapt lighting designed to protect the night's darkness and collaborate with other businesses and chambers of commerce to generate economic incentives that develop a common identity as it relates to the stars.

Creating programming (i.e., "Star Tours") can boost a local economy as a whole as visitors will spend their dollars with a wider number of vendors in town. Adventure travelers, such as astrotourists, are more interested in the experience than creature comforts. They are explorers who seek encounters that are singular, eccentric, and off-the-beaten paths. They hunt down the peculiar, distinctive, atypical, and idiosyncratic. Explorers blaze trails. This perchance allows for a greater range of offerings rather than the commonplace tourist considerations.

Housing

As they relate to dwellings, local ordinances vary from state-to-state, town-to-town, and temporary structures have their own specific requirements and must adhere to local ordinances. These suggestions are seasonal and not intended as permanent lodging.

Yurts are excellent choices for housing guests as they can be set up within hours, along with a wide variety of tents and teepees. Inflatable dwellings that are clear plastic globes large enough to house three to four people are now available. The latter is highly desirable as the guest can sleep in a big bubble that provides exceptional viewing conditions; however, it will require electricity to power the blower that keeps them inflated. Water can be trucked in, and wastewater trucked out. Electricity can be provided with portable generators or solar panels and cooking can be done with solar, propane, or butane stoves. "Glamping" (glamour meets camping) has a steep increase in interest in the travel market.

The "glamping" market in the United States is projected to reach $4.8 billion in revenue by 2025 at an estimated (Compound Annual Growth Rate) CAGR rate of 12.5 percent during that forecast period, according to a Market Watch report from October 6, 2019. The demand for cabins and safari tents is expected to grow 2.5 times over the next five years. Meanwhile, between 2014 and 2018, growth in U.S. camping households has steadily increased, from 71,500,000 homes in 2014 to nearly 80,000,000 last year. Millennials represent the fastest-growing demographic in new campers, with more diversity being represented among camping demographics.[6]

This insight into the projection of travel trends in combination with millennials seeking more experiential and eclectic travel options bodes well for astrotourism sites' purveyors. The amenities can range from primitive to rustic chic.

Booking platforms like Airbnb, VRBO, Trip Advisor, Glamping Hub, and the ubiquitous nature of social media gives a startup unprecedented access to a global audience for a fraction of the marketing costs once associated with launching an attraction or tourist destination. By gaining IDA certification, your destination is on a database and map maintained by IDA that allows travelers to find dark sky locations. Even without this certification, astrotourism is springing up around the world.

One location where it is having great success is in a remote region in South Africa, the Karoo, which is an arid to the semiarid geographic region of Eastern, Western, and Northern Cape provinces. The Karoo is best defined by its vegetation, which consists of assorted succulents and low scrub bushes spaced from one foot to several feet apart. The area is devoid of surface water, and its name is derived from the Khoisan word meaning "land of thirst."[7] With a landscape and weather similar to the American Southwest, the viewing conditions are highly favorable. The tourism and hospitality industry have bought into the Astro-theme, adopting space motifs and stellar imagery in the naming of their establishments, for example, Skitterland (Glitterland) Guesthouse, Jupiter Restaurant, Sterland (Starland), Southern Cross, and the Vlieënde Piering (the Flying Saucer).

Similar examples of thematic participation by a community can be found in Roswell, NM, the location of the "UFO Incident" back in 1947. Over half a century later, there are still shops called Alien Zone, Alien Invasion T's, and a UFO Museum. The town's website uses little alien head icons as the "pins" dropped on online maps. The Roswell city logo uses a flying saucer with a light beam shooting out of the bottom. Their baseball team is called the Invaders, and there is the Alien City Dragstrip. Alien eyes are painted onto downtown's historic street lamps and there is an annual UFO festival that attracts visitors from around the world.

As the Karoo is a "start-up" compared to the storied history of Roswell NM, they are still in the early stages of cultivating the area to

Figure 13.2 Space theme community participation—courtesy City of Roswell NM

accommodate visitors yet see the opening for economic development in an area that had little else to offer. Tourism enhancement is occurring due to various individual initiatives such as improved stakeholder relations, tour guide training, upgrading the quality and tarring of the roads to make the observatory more accessible to visitors, and producing arts and crafts as marketable products for tourists. Tour guiding and interpretation appear to be a desired feature, with some level of specialist experience and guidance essential to boost product delivery. The niche is perceived as being exorbitant, requiring quality equipment that is expensive and less portable.[2] The author takes exception to the last sentence and will demonstrate that equipment need not be costly to provide an exceptional experience for your guests.

Dark Sky Destination Appurtenances

The following are the author's suggestions to be considered a starting point. As technology changes, so will tourism. The offerings available in this writing will expand, evolve, develop, and become increasingly sophisticated as this new segment of the travel market continues to grow. More activities may be developed for a dark sky destination, and nothing puts it all into perspective like a Solar System Walk.

Solar System Walk

The fact is that the planets are mighty small, and the distances between them are ridiculously huge. To make any representation whose scale is true for the planet's sizes and distances, we must go outdoors.[9] This can be done to the scale of your choosing and demarcating the distances between the planets with our star Sol at the start of the walk. A version created by Guy Ottewell shows the comparison of distances and the planets' size ratio. It is called "The Thousand-Yard Model or, The Earth as a Peppercorn." At the start of your walk is the sun, and depending upon how much space you have, a path is demarcated by the planets as one walks away from the center of our solar system. The first plaque or sign would be Mercury, then Venus, Earth, and so on.

Figure 13.3 Sagan Planet Walk Marker

Source: Sciencenter, Ithaca, NY

The self-guided Chandler Solar System Walk at Veterans Oasis Park is a 2,500-foot path where one navigates around the lake along with a series of monuments and signs representing the sun, planets, and primary celestial objects—all placed at distances relative to the scale of the solar system. Each foot on the walk represents 1.5 million miles (2,414, 016 km), which means that the sun's distance to Earth is 62 (18.9m) feet along the walk—equivalent to the actual 93 million miles (149,668,992 km) between the two in space.[10]

Binoculars

Optical equipment like binoculars range from under a hundred to many thousands of dollars. Though it will enhance your offering, it is not obligatory to create an enjoyable, memorable evening for visitors. The viewers can see 25 or even 50 times more stars with a pair of binoculars than with the unaided eye.[11]

Binoculars are easy to use, do not require tripods (unless they are huge), pack small, light, and need little understanding to use them. As dark sky destinations are in remote locations, binoculars will serve double duty during the daytime for viewing landscapes, wildlife, and bird watching.

Telescopes

The price of telescopes has dramatically dropped, making them accessible for people who are on a minimal budget. Beginner telescopes are available for under $100 and can view the moon's surface, Mars, Jupiter's moon, Saturn's rings, and other celestial objects well beyond our solar system.[12] A telescope of much smaller diameter gave Galileo Galilei the ability to see enough of the night sky to change how we see the world so imagine what you can do? Sometimes amateur astronomers happen upon discoveries that rocked the scientific community.[13] There are 4-inch telescopes on the market for under $200 that will allow the viewer to see all of the planets in our solar system and distant objects like the Andromeda Galaxy and the Crab Nebula.

It is highly recommended that an equatorial mount is included as it allows the telescope to move in conjunction with the earth's rotation. Without an equatorial mount, the viewing object will continue to drift out of the frame. These beginner telescopes range from about 8.5–14 kilos. Though not small enough to throw around your neck like a pair of binoculars, they are built to pack into cases that are easy to transport. Telescopes can also be used for terrestrial viewing during the daytime as most dark sky destinations are in remote regions. The chances of seeing wildlife are more likely, and optical equipment can be utilized for remote viewing.

Pointers

A crucial piece of equipment is a pointer that ranges from twenty to a few hundred dollars. A flashlight with a capacity to focus the beam will work, and it is strongly urged to use a red lens to preserve night vision. A long thin stick with a keychain LED light on the end of it will also act as a pointer. Lasers that are powerful enough to see the beam are available online, and their price continues to drop while their power continues to rise. Stock a few extra laser pointers as they give your guests the efficiency to locate and point to stars as well. Once people experience lasers, they will find the length of their arm wholly inadequate when navigating the night sky.

My own experience of sharing the night revealed that people were every bit as interested in discovering how to find a constellation and learning their stories as having a view through a telescope of a celestial object.

Comfort Considerations

Winter provides some of the clearest skies and the brightest constellations. Hence, preparations are necessary to maintain your guests' well-being by having extra winter hats, scarves, mittens, blankets, ground-pads, hand warmers, hot-water bottles, and thermoses for hot beverages. A stationary or portable fire pit would also be most welcome, not only for the heat it provides but a gathering place for your guests. Everybody loves a warming fire as it not only feels good but connects us to our ancestral roots, and a sky ablaze with stars overhead awakens a primal sense of belonging to the cosmic picture. S'mores are optional. Drinking alcohol may make you feel warmer because the feeling is caused by blood rushing to the skin's surface. Alcohol also decreases sensitivity to cold, which in turn reduces the shivering process and deprives your body of extra heat. All of these factors actually increase the risk for hypothermia.[14]

Lighting Needs

To understand the lighting needs of the astrotourist, a brief on the anatomy of the eyeball is necessary. There are two types of cells in our eye that let us see. They are called rods and cones, and they are located in the retina at the back of the eye. The cones are highly sensitive to color and detail but do not function well in dim light. The rods are susceptible to light but cannot pick up very much detail.[15] Rods require 30 to 45 minutes or more of absolute darkness to attain 80 percent dark adaptation. Total dark adaptation can take many hours. While the rods in your eyes are far more light-sensitive than the cones, they can only discriminate between black and white.[16]

Viewing stars requires that one does not look directly at them but slightly askance to activate the rods in the retina's corners. A sleep mask can be put on to protect night vision before venturing out to prime the biological ocular sensors. After venturing into the night, the use of red light is of primary importance because if standard illumination is utilized, the eyes have to go through readjusting to the darkness. Various companies like Meade, Celestron, and Apetura make red lights specifically designed for stargazing and nighttime navigation.

The facility and housing area will require very specific luminaires if the lighting is to be used at all. Optimally, between 1,700k up to 2,200k to protect against light pollution and help maintain night vision. Under this kind of light, the eye's pupil does not constrict, thus allowing it to take in more light, and see past the luminaire to the stars overhead.

Outdoor light should be:

- Only be on when needed
- Only light the area that needs it
- Be no brighter than necessary
- Minimize blue light emissions
- Be fully shielded (pointing downward)[17]

Star charts and maps are essential as navigating the night sky without one is not possible. With a map, the viewer can find and identify planets, stars, major constellations, star clusters, nebulae, and even distant galaxies. Being able to open up a paper map that shows the entire sky has its advantages. Other alternatives are Star Guides that have movable discs nested on top of one another that are turned to the corresponding season.

Today there are also several smartphone applications. A limitation with these apps is their brightness and shifting one's gaze from the screen to the sky and back and again. It plays havoc with one's night vision and also due to their limited size, they can only be focused on a small portion of the night sky at a time. As most of the population is comfortable with their smartphones and the additional features that they possess, it is recommended to have guests download some star applications before their trip. Several are listed in the Resource section of this book.

Priming guests to do their "homework" before arrival will enhance their nighttime experience. Some gadgets and devices will help you capture the stars, the Moon, and more using your smartphone.[18] The most stunning deep space images are available online and can be downloaded onto a computer, tablet, or mobile phone.

To create a more textured and layered experience over the many hours under a night sky, consider a musical track to set the mood and tone. (See Music List) Think how much a soundtrack adds to a movie and how melodies become etched into our memory. Even silent movies were not silent as an organ or piano player was in the theater providing live music accompaniment. In 1977 the five tones, in the movie *Close Encounters of the Third Kind*, entered the public's consciousness and remained.[19] In the same year, Star Wars theme music also launched a generation and generations to follow into a galaxy far, far away. Like a scent can bring up a memory, so too can music played for the guests as they gaze into the night sky. Years later, hearing that tune will bring back the recollection of their time under the stars. A dark sky destination can host several different events or parties over the course of the year based on these celestial events.

Full Moon (varies)
New Moon (varies)
Winter/Summer Solstice (fixed)

Fall/Spring Equinox (fixed)
Cross-Quarter Days (fixed)
Meteor Shower (peaks fluctuate)
Star Party (anytime except when the moon is bright)
Zodiac Parties (12 Annually)

Though the highlight and purpose of astrotourism are to take in the night sky, a few items to have at a destination that can be appreciated during the daytime continues the theme as our sun is the closest star. Solar timepieces are a fascination for people even to this day. Most people know about sundials, but they rarely have exposure to them, and there is a rich history of these first devices for calculating time. Other types of astronomical devices for a destination might include:

*Sundials *Armillary spheres *Equinox Markers
*Analemmatic sundials *Orrery *Solar Walks *Solstice Markers

To close this chapter here is an arcane method that uses our closest star to tell time with nothing more than your hands. To estimate the time of day within 30 minutes or less, make a fist and, with an outstretched arm, place it on the horizon. The width of a fist will represent about one hour. Put the other fist on top of the first fist while keeping the first fist on the horizon. Keep stacking your fists, one on top of the other, until reaching the sun. Count backward from the time of sunset. If the sun sets at 8 pm and there are 6 stacked fists, one on top of the other, it will be about 2 p.m. In a tech-driven world, people are eager to learn that they can tell time as their forebears did going back to primitive cultures. With this, your guest has something in common, albeit simple by its nature, with ancient history.

CHAPTER 14

In Closing

When indoor plumbing arrived, we lost our connection to the night sky.
—Anonymous

Because this segment of the travel market is growing so rapidly and data is streaming in every day on ALAN's impact and what is being done worldwide to address it, a webpage has been created that will act as a compendium for this book. The growth is so astonishing that even in the time it took to write this, other developments have changed the night and landscape of countries. There are now curriculums being created in Namibia by astrophysicists to instruct locals to be star guides for the tourist trade, and astrostays are springing up in India.

The industrial revolution began in 1760, and in the course of 13 generations, civilization and modern humankind have untethered themselves from the planet and the night sky overhead. We do not know where our food comes from, and we are unaware of our carbon footprint; we do not realize the legacy that we are leaving with our consumption and the trail of refuse that litters the path behind us. However, our inextricable connection with Mother Earth is written into our DNA code and embedded into our psyche, and regardless of how big our cities become and how many people migrate away from rural settings, there is no escaping the call of the wild, the song of the night, the lure of the heavens and the stars that rest within its cloak of darkness. Journeys into a dark night heal and soothe a soul that has been strained and wearied by the pace of modern life, and this trend will continue to grow as people become aware of what awaits them under a canopy of eternity.

Case Studies

Questionnaires were sent out to Dark Sky locations around the world in 2019–20. The questions are posted below and a sample response is listed below. This will offer insight into anybody coordinating with a community, local stakeholders, and/or seeking to gain IDA accreditation to establish a certified dark sky destination. To view all Dark Sky certified destinations, visit the International Dark-Sky Association's website at darksky.org.

As this is a print publication, it was a choice to serve the reader better to set up a webpage that all of the hotlinks could be accessed as they pertain to the media, press, articles, television coverage, and programs at each one of these dark sky designated places. There was only room to include a few of the responses here; however, the others can be accessed at http:// mindofmarlin.com/literary/astrotourism/casestudies

1. What year did you apply for Dark Sky certification? What year was it granted?
2. What was the biggest obstacle in gaining IDA certification? How did you overcome these obstacles?
3. What lighting changes were made in your community/park to gain IDA certification?
4. Who in your community and the surrounding area has benefitted from your Dark Sky Certification? In what way?
5. Have you seen an increase in tourism since gaining your Dark Sky Certification? If yes, do you have data that you can share?
6. Is there any economic data after gaining Dark Sky certification that you can provide? (yes/no) Please explain.
7. Before moving towards Dark Sky certification, what were the circumstances that began the process? (i.e. complaints from residents, a decrease/increase insect/bird/wildlife counts, pedestrian/auto accidents, astronomy club input)

8. Has there been media coverage once you gained IDA certification? (yes/no) Please provide links to these, whether they be radio/television interviews, periodicals, magazines?
9. Did you engage the services of an outside consultant when retrofitting your community to be dark Sky compliant? (yes/no)
10. Is your community taking steps to market your Dark Sky community to visitors? If so, what?
11. Can you share some examples of your marketing materials?
12. Please provide any additional information that you think is relevant.

Eifel National Park

Eifel National Park is a 110-sq.-km conservation area in North Rhine-Westphalia, Germany, bordering Belgium and Rur Lake reservoir.

1. 2013—April 2014 (provisional) April 2019 final
2. Approximately two years due to illness. Hard work.
   Prove the tourist value. Work together with tourism organizations and with press and media.
   Prevent blue-rich light. Hundreds of hours talking with majors, lighting providers, and decision-makers.
3. In the park: lighting without output <500 nm. Full cut off, curfew. Around the park: many communities are already committed to installing FCO, </= 3000K, and switch off at midnight where possible.
4. The complete region of the National Park Eifel: Hotels, bread and breakfast, restaurants, and all others, who earn money through tourism. More guests, more profit for our providers of touristic offerings, because the Park is known to have a unique selling point: the starry night sky and landscapes.
5. About 5,000 bookings/per year for dedicated stargazing sessions. Many stand-alone amateur astronomers and nightscape photographers. I am just trying to collect some numbers regarding these kinds of visitors. We do not really know how many "stand-alone visitors" we have because many will visit the Dark Sky Park without notification. Nevertheless, we get feedback from hotels and B&Bs that they get more and more night owl visitors.

6. For me, as the owner and the Observatory operator, I do point to the approximately 5,000 bookings/per year of the two-hour stargazing sessions (15.00€ per adult / 7.50 € for kids and teens, free for a child younger than 12 years).

7. Definitely my idea (*the respondent*) and my passion for bringing back stargazing to people. Most regional partners need to be convinced about the status of light pollution and dark skies. The learning curve was different. The touristic advantages are still important leverage.

8. This collection is not complete; However, we see about 300–500 hits per year:
http://sterne-ohne-grenzen.de/medien-echo
Eifel National Park Administration collects newspaper articles and divides them into specific topics. There were numerous newspaper clippings where International Dark Sky Park Eifel National Park was mentioned:
2018—366 articles
2017—630 articles
2016—87 articles
2015—288 articles

9. Yes: I was the consultant in many cases, but also some regional lighting providers support the dark skies mission, and we work together.

10. Yes. They provide observation locations, and they organize local events like exhibitions and stargazing incentives. See https://www.sternenregion-eifel.de/projekt/ausstellung/

11. Please see: http://www.sterne-ohne-grenzen.de/nachhaltiger-astro-tourismus/werbung-f%C3%BCr-die-sternenreiche-nacht/
Outreach activities like "Culture at Night" or "Star Week" with different offerings like night guide tours through communities and cities, night walks, nature observations (bat, beaver), and stargazing, of course. Eifel National Park promotes the International Dark Sky Park and the stargazing programs; see this:
• https://nationalpark-eifel.de/en/experience-national-park/dark-sky-park/
• https://nationalpark-eifel.de/de/nationalpark-erleben/veranstaltungen/

12. We need more regulation, an EU-wide law against light pollution.

Music List

These selections are based on both relevances of words in the title of the song or the ambiance it would create under the magical canopy of a star-studded sky. The genres are bluegrass, standards, rock, jazz, classical, electronica, and movie soundtracks. Have fun creating your own playlists. It is prudent and the right thing to pay BMI/ASCAP the royalty fee, which is distributed to the artists whose works you are using. The annual fee is the modest sum of $250 dollars, which is well worth the price of the audioscape that will greatly enrich the evening's experience. There would be no such thing a complete list and this is to be consider but a starting point.

Fly Me to the Moon—Frank Sinatra
Stardust Memory—Artie Shaw
Moon River—Andy Williams
It's Only a Paper Moon—Ella Fitzgerald
Blue Moon of Kentucky—Bill Monroe
Blue Moon—The Marcels
Amore—Dean Martin
Swinging on a Star—Bing Crosby
Across the Universe—The Beatles
I'll Follow the Sun—The Beatles
Good Morning Starshine—Oliver
Rocket Man—Elton John
Moon Shadow—Cat Stevens
Dancing in the Moonlight—King Harvest
Till There Was You—Meredith Wilson
You're A Sky Full of Stars—Coldplay
Total Eclipse of the Moon—Engima
Lucky Star—Madonna
Drops of Jupiter—Train
All of the Stars—Ed Sheeran
Dark Star—The Grateful Dead

Space Truckin'—Deep Purple
Nights in White Satin—The Moody Blues
We are all made of Stars—Moby
Space Cowboy—Steve Miller
Riders on the Storm—The Doors
Walking on the Moon—Cas Haley
Space Oddity—David Bowie
Andromeda—Paul Weller
Bad Moon Rising—Creedence Clearwater Revival
Total Eclipse of the Heart—Bonnie Tyler
Stars and Planets—Liz Phair
Man on the Moon—REM
Another Star—Stevie Wonder
Blue Moon—Beck
Everyone's Gone to the Moon—Johnathan King
Dark Side of the Moon—Pink Floyd (Album)
Shining Star— The Manhattans
Moondance—Van Morrison
Starman—David Bowie
The Sun—Brenda Carlisle
Yellow Moon—Neville Brothers
Planetary Unfolding—Michael Stearns
Harlem Nocturne—Earl Klugh
Nocturne Op. 9 No. 1—Frederick Chopin
Nocturne Op. 9 No. 2—Frederick Chopin
Moonlight Sonata—Beethoven
Air on the G String—J.S. Bach
Gregorian Chants
The Planets—Gustav Holst
In the Middle of Night—Billy Joel
Twinkle, Twinkle Little Star—Jane Taylor
Fanfare for the Common Man—Aaron Copland
Star Trek Theme—John Williams
X-Files Theme—Mark Snow
Tubular Bells—Mark Oldfield
Solo Piano Music—Philip Glass

Oxygene—Jean-Michel Jarre

Phaedra—Tangerine Dream

Thus Spake Zarathustra—Richard Strauss

Soundtracks to these Movies:

Blade Runner

Star Trek

Star Wars

2001 A Space Odyssey

Interstellar

Alien(s)

Ghost in a Shell

Moon

Any science fiction or space themed movie.

Notes

Chapter 1

1. Falchi, et al. (2016).
2. Wall (2017).

Chapter 2

1. Marquès (2020).
2. Machando (2014), www.grammarist.com/usage/connect-the-dots-and-join-the-dots (accessed September 24, 2020).
3. Anderberg (2019).

Chapter 3

1. Dann (1981).
2. Hill (2019).
3. Source: statistica.com.
4. Lowrey (2019).
5. Airbnb.com (2018).
6. Williams (1988).
7. Mitchell and Gallaway (2019).
8. Hunter and Crawford (1991).
9. Mitchell and Gallaway (2019), p. 27.

Chapter 4

1. https://advances.sciencemag.org/content/2/6/e1600377
2. https://globalnews.booking.com/reveals key findings from its 2019 sustainable travel report/retrieved 2-8-2020.
3. *ICAO.*
4. (Sumers 2019).
5. https://britannica.com/biography/Thomas-Hiram-Holding
6. (Holding 1908).
7. (Simkins 2020).
8. (Houghton 2018).
9. *Mobile Phone Ownership Over Time* (2019).
10. Thenumbers.com/movies/franchise/Star-Wars
11. (Levine 2019).

12. (Manning 1996).
13. *The New World Atlas of Artificial Night Sky Brightness.*

Chapter 5

1. https://science.ksc.nasa.gov/mirrors/gsfc/omni/eclipse99/pages/amazing.
html.
2. (Wood 2020).
3. https://lunarphasepro.com/full-moon-names/retrieved 11-30-2020.
4. NASA: Solar Systems—Comets and Meteors.
5. (Lunsford 2018).
6. (Howell 2019).
7. *What is a Solar Cycle?*
8. (Feldstein 1986).
9. NASA.
10. *Northern Light Trips and Tips.*
11. *Glass Igloos.*
12. (Pöyry n.d.).
13. Airbnb Office of Healthy Tourism.
14. International Dark Sky Places.

Chapter 6

1. http://zpub.com/sf/history/sfh-cc.html
2. NASA; Mission anniversary.
3. (Stephen 2020).
4. (Kokorich 2020).
5. Foust (January 28, 2002); (Lewis 2021).
6. https://space-affairs.com/en
7. (Pushkar 2002).
8. https://incredible-adventures.com/
9. https://thespaceperspective.com/
10. (Schneider 2020).
11. (Kaplan 2013).
12. (Carter 2019).
13. (Wall 2020).
14. https://virgingalactic.com/mission/
15. https://spacex.com/vehicles/starship/index.html/
16. (Harwood 2019).
17. (Wilson 2010).
18. http://gatewayspaceport.com/the-gateway/

Chapter 7

1. (Boyle 2017).
2. (Flint 2019).
3. (Gernon 2017).
4. (Bromwich 2017).
5. (Carter 2020).
6. (Joe Rao 2020).
7. (Stimac 2019).
8. (Carter July 2020).
9. https://britannica.com/list/the-sun-was-eaten-6-ways-cultures-have-explained-eclipses
10. (Farrell 2017).
11. https://eclipse.aas.org/eclipse-america/when-where

Chapter 8

1. https://sciencefriday.com/articles/science-diction-sun
2. (Iqbal et al. 2009).
3. (Faramarzi 2020).
4. https://newgrange.com/winter_solstice.html
5. https://smithsonianmag.com/smart-news/fall-equinox-secret-pyramids-near-perfect-alignment-180968223/
6. (Jarus 2018).
7. https://cancunadventure.net/chichenitza-equinox/
8. https://britannica.com/topic/Stonehenge
9. https://historicenvironment.scot/visit-a-place/places/maeshowe-chambered-cairn/
10. https://mayanpeninsula.com/ball-court-in-uxmal/
11. https://whc.unesco.org/en/list/353
12. https://www2.hao.ucar.edu/Education/SolarAstronomy/sun-dagger
13. https://wmf.org/project/chankillo
14. https://whc.unesco.org/en/list/198
15. https://whc.unesco.org/en/list/274/
16. https://almanac.com/content/five-ancient-sites-aligned-solstice-and-equinox
17. https://guidememalta.com/en/experience-the-amazing-equinox-phenomena-at-hagar-qim-mnajdra-temples
18. https://whc.unesco.org/en/list/668; retrieved 8-17-2020
19. https://sunearthday.nasa.gov/2005/locations/angkorwat.htm retrieved 8-23-2020
20. https://ancient.eu/Hovenweep/ retrieved 8-26-2020
21. Manek n.d.

Chapter 9

1. https://eaae-astronomy.org/find-a-sundial/short-history-of-sundials (accessed December 8, 2020).
2. https://britannica.com/technology/sundial (accessed August 19, 2020).
3. Scott (1872).
4. https://turtlebay.org/sundial-bridge (accessed November 29, 2020).
5. https://jantarmantar.org/learn/observatories/instruments/samrat/index.html (accessed August 21, 2020).
6. http://stpetersbasilica.info/Exterior/Obelisk/Obelisk.htm (accessed October 25, 2020).
7. The secrets of the Vatican Obelisk in St. Peter's Square (2018) https://vox-mundi.eu/secrets-vatican-obelisk/(accessed August 24, 2020).
8. https://atlasobscura.com/places/astronomical-clock-besancon (accessed August 26, 2020).
9. https://afar.com/places/prague-astronomical-clock-prague(accessed   August 22, 2020).
10. https://atlasobscura.com/places/horologium-mirabile-lundense(accessed August 24, 2020).
11. https://atlasobscura.com/places/wells-cathedral-clock (accessed August 23, 2020).
12. https://buyoya.com/gros-horloge-gothic-old-clock-rouen-france (accessed August 24, 2020).
13. https://bern.com/en/detail/berns-clock-tower-zytglogge (accessed November 19, 2020).
14. https://atlasobscura.com/places/torre-dell-orologio-venice-clock-tower (accessed August 24, 2020).
15. Barry (2014) https://italymagazine.com/featured-story/venices-clock-tower-masterpiece-technology-and-engineering (accessed August 25, 2020).
16. https://italymagazine.com/dual-language/discover-cremonas-torrazzo-italys-tallest-bell-tower (accessed August 24, 2020).
17. https://atlasobscura.com/places/the-zimmer-clock-tower-and-museum-lier-belgium (accessed August 22, 2020).

Chapter 10

1. http://euskyroute.eu
2. http://euskyroute.eu/wp-content/uploads/2015/11/bulgaria.pdf.
3. https://chile-travel-and-news.com/2019/10/astronomical-tourism-in-chile.html.
4. Agencia EFE Santiago (2015) https://efe.com/efe/english/technology/chile-to-host-70-pct-of-global-astronomical-infrastructure-by-2020/50000267-2587084

5. https://astronomictourism.com/tourist-observatories-chile.html.

6. https://astronomictourism.com/major-astronomy-projects.html.

7. https://almaobservatory.org/en/press-releases/astronomers-capture-first-image-of-a-black-hole/

8. https://france-voyage.com/tourism/sundials-hautes-alpes-1353.htm.

9. https://shadowspro.com/photos/besancon/pasteur.html.

10. (Allport 2003).

11. http://sundials.co/~houston.htm.

12. https://sites.google.com/site/northwestsundials/seattle-sundial-trail

13. Londonist.

14. https://nasa.gov/content/goddard/hubble-s-messier-catalog

Chapter 11

1. http://sci-news.com/othersciences/anthropology/graecopithecus-freybergi-hominin-04888.html.

2. (Berna et al. 2012).

3. https://britannica.com/science/kelvin

4. (Josephson 1959).

5. https://nigms.nih.gov/education/pages/factsheet_circadianrhythms.asp

6. https://ntp.niehs.nih.gov/events/webinars-workshops/2016/alan/index.html?utm_source=direct&utm_medium=prod&utm_campaign=ntpgolinks&utm_term=workshop_alan

7. https://anses.fr/en/content/leds-blue-light 13/08/2019

8. https://darksky.org/light-pollution/night-sky-heritage/

9. (Drake 2019).

10. https://facebook.com/groups/155084901640186/

11. https://visioneyeinstitute.com.au/eyematters/night-vision/

12. https://ama-assn.org/press-center/press-releases/ama-adoptsguidance-reduce-harm-high-intensity-street-lights

13. (Chaney 2002).

14. https://audubon.org/https://audubonorgmenuconservation/existing-lights-out-programs

Chapter 12

1. Membery, York First Newspaper Horoscope.

2. (Herman 1998).

3. (Rossiter 2002).

4. http://stargazing.net/david/constel/starnames.html.

5. (Hamid 2007).

6. https://britannica.com/biography/Johann-Bayer

7. https://britannica.com/topic/Perseus-Greek-mythology

8. (Crossland 2017).

9. https://australiamyland.com.au/outback.html.

10. https://didjshop.com/shop1/AbCulturecart.html.

11. (Norris n.d.).

12. http://ianridpath.com/startales/bayer%20southern.htm.

13. https://maritiemdigitaal.nl/index.cfm?event=search.getdetail&id=101004 022

14. (Rao 2013).

Chapter 13

1. (Ingle 2010).

2. (Laeticia et al. 2020).

3. (Camp 2012).

4. Turning off street lights does not lead to more crime or accidents—study (2015).

5. (Morrow et al. 2000).

6. (McNulty 2019).

7. https://britannica.com/place/Karoo

9. (Ottewell 1989).

10. https://visitchandler.com/listings/chandler-solar-system-walk-at-veterans-oasis-park/783/

11. (Brody 2018).

12. https://likehubble.com/best-starter-telescopes-for-beginners

13. (Heussner 2009).

14. (7 Busted Cold Weather Myths 2017).

15. UCSB ScienceLine, http://scienceline.ucsb.edu/getkey.php?key=923

16. Tips For Improving Night Vision.

17. Outdoor Lighting Basics.

18. (Carter 2019).

19. https://ars-nova.com/Theory%20Q&A/Q35.html.

References

"International Dark Sky Places." https://darksky.org/our-work/conservation/idsp/ (accessed February 14, 2020).

"Northern Light Trips and Tips." https://tourradar.com/f/northern-lights (accessed January 13, 2020).

"What is a Solar Cycle? NASA." https://spaceplace.nasa.gov/solar-cycles/en/ (accessed February 26, 2020).

7 Busted Cold Weather Myths. 2017. https://stlukeshealth.org/resources/7-busted-cold-weather-myths (accessed September 1, 2020).

Agencia EFE Santiago. 2015. https://efe.com/efe/english/technology/chile-to-host-70-pct-of-global-astronomical-infrastructure-by,2020./50000267-2587084 (accessed October 30, 2020).

Airbnb Office of Healthy Tourism. n.d. https://airbnbcitizen.com/officeofhealthytourism (accessed February 23, 2020).

Airbnb.com. 2018. (accessed February 28, 2020).

Allport, S. 2003. *Solar-Powered Timekeeping in Paris*. NY Times https://nytimes.com/2003/03/16/travel/solar-powered-timekeeping-in-paris.html; (accessed October 28, 2020).

Anderberg, J. 2019. "15 Constellations Every Man Should Know." https://artofmanliness.com/articles/ (accessed May 8, 2020).

Berna, G., H. Brink, and C. Bamford. 2012. "Microstratigraphic evidence of in situ fire in the Acheulean strata of Wonderwerk Cave, Northern Cape province, South Africa." https://doi.org/10.1073/pnas.1117620109 (accessed February 18, 2020).

Boyle, R. 2017. "The Largest Mass Migration to See a Natural Event Is Coming." https://theatlantic.com/science/archive/2017/08/the-greatest-mass-migration-in-american-history/535734/ (accessed September 9, 2020).

Brody, D.S. 2018. "How to Choose Binoculars for Astronomy and Skywatching." https://space.com/27404-binoculars-buying-guide.html (accessed September 2, 2020).

Bromwich, J.E. 2017. "215 Million Americans Watched the Solar Eclipse." https://nytimes.com/2017/09/27/science/solar-eclipse-record-numbers.html (accessed September 11, 2020).

Camp, J. 2012. "Decisions are Largely Emotional, Not Logical." https://bigthink.com/experts-corner/decisions-are-emotional-not-logical-the-neuroscience-behind-decision-making (accessed March 15, 2020).

Carter, J. 2019. "Best Gadgets to Turn Your Smartphone into an Astrophotography Camera." https://skyatnightmagazine.com/top-astronomy-kit/best-gadgets-turn-smartphone-into-astrophotography-camera (accessed September 4, 2020).

Carter, J. 2019. "Virgin Galactic Everything You Need To Know." https://techradar.com/news/virgin-galactic-everything-you-need-to-know (accessed August 17, 2020).

Carter, J. 2020. "50 Million People May Gather For the 'Greater American Eclipse.'" https://forbes.com/sites/jamiecartereurope/2020/04/07/50-million-people-may-gather-for-the-greater-american-eclipse-the-most-watched-in-history/#19338fe76ce9 (accessed September 11, 2021).

Carter, J. July 2020. "Why 2024's 'Greater American Eclipse' is Already a Massive Event." https://whenisthenexteclipse.com/2024-greater-american-eclipse-a-massive-event/ (accessed September 2, 2020).

Chaney, W.R. 2002. "Purdue University, Forestry, and Natural Resources, FAQ 17." 4 https://extension.purdue.edu/extmedia/FNR/FNR-FAQ-17.pdf (accessed February 16, 2020).

Crossland, J. 2017. "Tourist Want More Experiences When They Travel." https://entrepreneurial-life.today/tourists-want-more-experiences/ (accessed February 29, 2020).

Dann, G.M.S. 1981. "Tourist Motivation an Appraisal." *Annals of Tourism Research* 8, no. 2, 187–219. https://doi.org/10.1177/004728758202100282 (accessed December 28, 2020).

Drake, N. 2019. "Our Nights are Getting Brighter, and Earth is Paying the Price." National Geographic (accessed February 20, 2020).

Falchi, F., P. Cinzano, D. Duriscoe, C.C. Kyba, C.D. Elvidge, K. Baugh, and R. Furgoni. 2016. "The New World Atlas of Artificial Night Sky Brightness." *Science Advances* 2, no. 6, advances.sciencemag.org/content/2/6/e1600377 (accessed December 3, 2019).

Faramarzi, S. 2020. https://middleeasteye.net/discover/what-nowruz-explained-persian-new-year-celebrated (accessed August 19, 2020).

Farrell, P.A. 2017. "Solar Eclipse Fanatics Already Trying to Find Prime Locations for the 2024 Event." https://freep.com/story/news/local/michigan/2017/08/22/solar-eclipse-prime-locations-2024/591455001/ (accessed October 11, 2020).

Feldstein, Y.I. 1986. "A Quarter Century with the Auroral Oval." https://doi.org/10.1029/EO067i040p00761-02 (accessed March 15, 2020).

Feldstein, Y.I. 1986. "A Quarter Century with the Auroral Oval." https://doi.org/10.1029/EO067i040p00761-02 (accessed March 15, 2020).

Flint, J. 2019. "Travel Will Change for the Better this Year—Here is How." https://nationalgeographic.com/travel/lists/top-travel-trends-this-year/ (accessed September 10, 2020).

Foust, J. January 28, 2002. "Dennis Tito Cautious About Space Tourism Future." Smithsonian Magazine; (accessed August, 12, 2020).

Gatty, M.S. 1872. *The Book of Sun* Dials, 22–23. London: George Bell & Sons.

Gernon, D. 2017. "Once in a Lifetime Solar Eclipse is a Bonanza for Hotels, Airlines." https://cnbc.com/2017/07/26/once-in-a-lifetime-solar-eclipse-is-a-bonanza-for-hotels-airlines.html (accessed January 17, 2021).

Glass Igloos, https://archello.com/project/glass-igloos (accessed January 15, 2020).

grammarist.com/usage/connect-the-dots-and-join-the-dots (accessed August 24, 2020).

Hamid, Z.A. 2007. "Arabic Star Names: A Treasure of Knowledge Shared by the World." https://muslimheritage.com/arabic-star-names (accessed November 4, 2019).

Harwood, W. 2019. "Blue Origin Launches New Shepard Rocket With NASA Payloads." https://cbsnews.com/news (accessed August 20, 2020).

Herman, R. 1998. "How fast is the Earth Moving?" https://scientificamerican.com/article/how-fast-is-the-earth-mov/ (accessed November 27, 2019).

Heussner, Ki Mae. 2009. "7 Great Discoveries by Amateur Astronomers." https://abcnews.go.com/Technology/Space/story?id=8221167&page=1 (accessed September 3, 2020).

Hill, D. 2019. "Star Struck Township." North Canterbury News, https://ncnews.co.nz/community/ (accessed November 10, 2019).

Holding, T.H. 1908. *The Camper's Handbook*. Simpkin, Marshall, Hamilton, Kent.

Houghton, M. 2018. "Why Camping is Rising in Popularity Especially Among Millennials." *Forbes*, https://forbes.com/sites (accessed February 2, 2020).

Howell, E. 2019. "Chelyabinsk Meteor Wake up Call For Earth." https://space.com/33623-chelyabinsk-meteor-wake-up-call-for-earth.html (accessed October 22, 2020).

Howell, E. 2019. "Chelyabinsk Meteor Wake up Call For Earth." https://space.com/33623-chelyabinsk-meteor-wake-up-call-for-earth.html (accessed October 22, 2020).

http://euskyroute.eu (accessed November 2, 2020).

http://euskyroute.eu/wp-content/uploads/2015/11/bulgaria.pdf (accessed November 1, 2020).

http://gatewayspaceport.com/the-gateway/ (accessed November 28, 2020).

http://ianridpath.com/startales/bayer%20southern.htm (accessed October 24, 2020).

http://sci-news.com/othersciences/anthropology/graecopithecus-freybergi-hominin-04888.html (accessed February 18, 2020).

http://stargazing.net/david/constel/starnames.html (accessed October 25, 2019).

http://stpetersbasilica.info/Exterior/Obelisk/Obelisk.htm (accessed October 25, 2020).

http://sundials.co/~houston.htm (accessed October 28, 2020).

http://zpub.com/sf/history/sfh-cc.html (accessed August 16, 2020).

https://advances.sciencemag.org/content/2/6/e1600377 (accessed February 10, 2020).

https://afar.com/places/prague-astronomical-clock-prague (accessed August 22, 2020).

https://almanac.com/content/five-ancient-sites-aligned-solstice-and-equinox (accessed August 21, 2020).

https://almaobservatory.org/en/press-releases/astronomers-capture-first-image-of-a-black-hole/ (accessed November 1, 2020).

https://ama-assn.org/press-center/press-releases/ama-adopts   guidance-reduce-harm-high-intensity-street-lights June 14 2016 (accessed February 17, 2020).

https://ancient.eu/Hovenweep/ (accessed August 26, 2020).

https://anses.fr/en/content/leds-blue-light 13/08/2019 (accessed February 18, 2020).

https://ars-nova.com/Theory%20Q&A/Q35.html; (accessed September 5, 2020).

https://astronomictourism.com/major-astronomy-projects.html (accessed October 29, 2020).

https://astronomictourism.com/tourist-observatories-chile.html (accessed October 29, 2020).

https://atlasobscura.com/places/astronomical-clock-besancon (accessed August 26, 2020).

https://atlasobscura.com/places/horologium-mirabile-lundense (accessed August 24, 2020).

https://atlasobscura.com/places/the-zimmer-clock-tower-and-museum-lier-belgium (accessed August 22, 2020).

https://atlasobscura.com/places/torre-dell-orologio-venice-clock-tower (accessed August 24, 2020).

https://atlasobscura.com/places/wells-cathedral-clock (accessed August 23, 2020).

https://audubon.org/https://audubonorgmenuconservation/existing-lights-out-programs (accessed August 12, 2020).

https://australiamyland.com.au/outback.html (accessed February 29, 2020).

https://bern.com/en/detail/berns-clock-tower-zytglogge (accessed November 19, 2020).

https://britannica.com/biography/Johann-Bayer; (accessed December 3, 2019).

https://britannica.com/biography/Thomas-Hiram-Holding, (accessed November 19, 2020).

https://britannica.com/list/the-sun-was-eaten-6-ways-cultures-have-explained-eclipses (accessed October 11, 2020).

https://britannica.com/place/Karoo (accessed September 2, 2020).

https://britannica.com/science/kelvin (accessed September 1, 2020).

https://britannica.com/technology/sundial (accessed August 19, 2020).

https://www.britannica.com/biography/Yuri-Gagarin; Retrieved 8 December, 2020.

https://britannica.com/topic/Perseus-Greek-mythology; (accessed December 15, 2020).

https://britannica.com/topic/Stonehenge (accessed August 19, 2020).

https://buyoya.com/gros-horloge-gothic-old-clock-rouen-france (accessed August 24, 2020).

https://cancunadventure.net/chichenitza-equinox/ (accessed August 20, 2020).

https://chile-travel-and-news.com/2019/10/astronomical-tourism-in-chile.html (accessed October 28, 2020).

https://darksky.org/light-pollution/night-sky-heritage/ (accessed February 17, 2020).

https://didjshop.com/shop1/AbCulturecart.html (accessed March 1, 2020).

https://eaae-astronomy.org/find-a-sundial/short-history-of-sundials (accessed August 12, 2020).

https://eclipse.aas.org/eclipse-america/when-where (accessed October 15, 2020).

https://facebook.com/groups/155084901640186/

https://france-voyage.com/tourism/sundials-hautes-alpes-1353.htm (accessed October 28, 2020).

https://globalnews.booking.com/reveals key findings from its 2019 sustainable travel report/ (accessed February 8, 2020).

https://guidememalta.com/en/experience-the-amazing-equinox-phenomena-at-hagar-qim-mnajdra-temples (accessed August 21, 2020).

https://historicenvironment.scot/visit-a-place/places/maeshowe-chambered-cairn/ (accessed August 18, 2020).

https://incredible-adventures.com/ (accessed August 4, 2020).

https://italymagazine.com/dual-language/discover-cremonas-torrazzo-italys-tallest-bell-tower (accessed August 24, 2020).

https://jantarmantar.org/learn/observatories/instruments/samrat/index.html (accessed August 21, 2020).

https://likehubble.com/best-starter-telescopes-for-beginners (accessed September 3, 2020).

https://lunarphasepro.com/full-moon-names/ (accessed November 30, 2020).

https://lunarphasepro.com/full-moon-names/ (accessed November 30, 2020).

https://maritiemdigitaal.nl/index.cfm?event=search.getdetail&id=101004022 (accessed October 24, 2020).

https://mayanpeninsula.com/ball-court-in-uxmal/ (accessed August 17, 2020).

https://nasa.gov/content/goddard/hubble-s-messier-catalog (accessed October 26, 2020).

https://newgrange.com/winter_solstice.html; (accessed August 19, 2020).

https://nigms.nih.gov/education/pages/factsheet_circadianrhythms.asp (accessed February 15, 2020).

https://ntp.niehs.nih.gov/events/webinars-workshops/2016/alan/index.html?utm_source=direct&utm_medium=prod&utm_campaign=ntpgolinks&utm_term=workshop_alan (accessed February 19, 2020).

https://sciencefriday.com/articles/science-diction-sun (accessed August 15, 2020).

https://shadowspro.com/photos/besancon/pasteur.html; (accessed October 28, 2020).

https://sites.google.com/site/northwestsundials/seattle-sundial-trail (accessed October 27, 2020).

https://smithsonianmag.com/smart-news/fall-equinox-secret-pyramids-near-perfect-alignment-180968223/ (accessed August 21, 2020).

https://space-affairs.com/en (accessed August 3, 2020).

https://spacex.com/vehicles/starship/index.html/ (accessed August 13, 2020).

https://sunearthday.nasa.gov/2005/locations/angkorwat.htm (accessed August 23, 2020).

https://thespaceperspective.com/ (accessed August 7, 2020).

https://turtlebay.org/sundial-bridge (accessed November 29, 2020).

https://virgingalactic.com/mission/ (accessed August 9, 2020).

https://visioneyeinstitute.com.au/eyematters/night-vision/ 2017 (accessed February 17, 2020).

https://visitchandler.com/listings/chandler-solar-system-walk-at-veterans-oasis-park/783/ (accessed October 24, 2020).

https://whc.unesco.org/en/list/198 (accessed August 18, 2020).

https://whc.unesco.org/en/list/274/ (accessed August 19, 2020).

https://whc.unesco.org/en/list/353 (accessed August 15, 2020).

https://whc.unesco.org/en/list/668 (accessed August 17, 2020).

https://wmf.org/project/chankillo (accessed August 16, 2020).

https://www2.hao.ucar.edu/Education/SolarAstronomy/sun-dagger (accessed August 14, 2020).

Hunter, T., and D.L. Crawford. 1991. "Economics of Light Pollution." *International Astronomical Union Colloquium* 112, 89–96. doi:10.1017/S0252921100003778

ICAO Global Environmental Trends- Present and Future Aircraft Noise and Emissions; International Civil Aviation Organization A40-WP/54 EX/21 5-7-2019 (accessed February 15, 2020).

Ingle, M.K. 2010. "Making the Most of 'nothing': Astro-Tourism, the Sublime, and the Karoo as a 'Space Destination,'." *Transformation Critical Perspectives on Southern Africa* 74, no. 1, 87–111 doi: 10.1353/trn.2010.0013, https://researchgate.net/publication/236782379_Making_the_most_of_%27nothing%27_astro-tourism_the_Sublime_and_the_Karoo_as_a_%27space_destination%27 (accessed March 14, 2020).

International Dark Sky Places. n.d. https://darksky.org/our-work/conservation/idsp/ (accessed February 14, 2020).

Iqbal, N., M.N. Vahia, T. Masood, and A. Ahmad. 2009. "Some Early Astronomical Sites in the Kashmir Region." *Journal of Astronomical History and Heritage* (ISSN 1440-2807) 12, no. 1, pp. 61–65.

Jacobs, L., E.A. Du Preez, and F. Fairer-Wessels. 2020. "To Wish Upon a Star: Exploring Astro Tourism as a Vehicle for Sustainable Rural Development." *Development Southern Africa* 37, no. 1, 87–104, Doi: 10.1080/0376835X.2019.1609908 (accessed March 14, 2020).

Jarus, O. 2018. "Secret to Great Pyramid's Near-Perfect Alignment Possibly Found." https://livescience.com/61799-great-pyramid-near-perfect-alignment.html (accessed December 5, 2020).

Joe, R. 2020. "We're T-Minus 4 Years to the Next Great American Solar Eclipse in 2024." https://space.com/great-american-solar-eclipse-2024-four-years-away.html (accessed October 9, 2020).

Josephson, M. 1959. *"Edison" McGraw Hill,* 255. New York. OCLC 485621. ISBM 0-07-033046-8

Julien, M. 2017. "Stargazing Keeps Tourism Looking Up." https://phys.org/news/2017-03-stargazing-tourism.html, (accessed March 4, 2020).

Julien, M. 2017. "Stargazing Keeps Tourism Looking Up." https://phys.org/news/2017-03-stargazing-tourism.html (accessed March 4, 2020).

Kaplan, K. 2013. "Did Neil Armstrong Really Say, 'That's One Small Step For a Man'?" *Los Angeles Times*; https://latimes.com/science/sciencenow; (accessed August 17, 2020).

Kokorich, M. 2020. "Private Space Industrialization Is Here." https://techcrunch.com/2020/08/18/private-space-industrialization-is-here/ (accessed August 18, 2020).

Levine, A. 2019. " 'Star Wars': How to have fun using the Force at Disneyland's Galaxy Edge Land." USA Today, https://usatoday.com/story/travel/experience/america/theme-parks/ (accessed February 21, 2020).

Lewis, S. 2021. "CBS News." https://cbsnews.com/news/axion-space-ax1-crew-55-million-first-private-mission-international-space-station/ (accessed February 2, 2021).

Lillie, B. 2014. https://italymagazine.com/featured-story/venices-clock-tower-masterpiece-technology-and-engineering (accessed August 25, 2020).

Londonist, https://londonist.com/london/great-outdoors/sundials-of-london (accessed November 2, 2020).

Lowrey, A. 2019. "Too Many People Want to Travel." *The Atlantic*, https://theatlantic.com/ideas/archive (accessed March 4, 2019).

Lunsford, R.D. 2018. "What Are Meteors and Why do They Glow?" https://astroleague.org/al/obsclubs/meteor/metwhat.html, (accessed February 23, 2020).

Lunsford, R.D. 2018. "What Are Meteors and Why do They Glow?" https://astroleague.org/al/obsclubs/meteor/metwhat.html (accessed February 23, 2020).

Machando, A. 2014. "How Millennials are Changing Travel." *The Atlantic*, https://theatlantic.com/international/archive/2014/06 (accessed May 13, 2020).

Manek, I. n.d. https://stargazingmumbai.in/5-archaeo-astronomical-sites-in-india-that-you-must-visit/ (accessed August 26, 2020).

Manning, J.G. 1996. "The Role of Planetariums in Astronomy Education." 80. https://ui.adsabs.harvard.edu/abs/1996ASPC...89...80M/abstract (accessed January 25, 2020).

Marquès, G. n.d. *Understanding Golden Hour, Blue Hour and Twilight*, http://photopills.com (accessed March 4, 2020).

McNulty, M. 2019. "Why is Glamping Taking Over the Travel Industry?" https://foxbusiness.com/lifestyle/the-economics-and-phenomena-of-glamping-and-why-its-taking-over-the-travel-industry (accessed March 25, 2020).

Membery, "York First Newspaper Horoscope." https://astrologysource.com/astrology-articles/first-newspaper-horoscopes/ (accessed December 10, 2020).

Mitchell, D., and T. Gallaway. 2019. "Dark Sky Tourism: Economic Impacts on the Colorado Plateau Economy, USA." *Tourism Review*, p. 22, (accessed March 15, 2020).

Mitchell, D., and T. Gallaway. 2019. "Dark Sky Tourism: Economic Impacts on the Colorado Plateau Economy, USA." *Tourism Review*, p. 27 (accessed March 15, 2020).

Mobile Phone Ownership Over Time. 2019. Fact Sheet; Pew Research Center https://pewresearch.org/internet/fact-sheet/mobile/ (accessed February 12, 2020).

Morrow, E.N., and S.A. Hutton. 2000. *The Chicago Alley Lighting Project: Final Evaluation Report*. Research and Analysis Unit-Illinois Criminal Justice Information Authority. https://ncjrs.gov/App/publications/Abstract.aspx?id=188494 (accessed March 24, 2020).

NASA, ACE https://science.nasa.gov/missions/ace (accessed February 25, 2020).

NASA, ACE. https://science.nasa.gov/missions/ace (accessed February 25, 2020).

NASA: Solar Systems—Comets and Meteors. https://solarsystem.nasa.gov/asteroids-comets-and-meteors/overview/ (accessed December 13, 2009).

NASA: Solar Systems—Comets and Meteors. https://solarsystem.nasa.gov/asteroids-comets-and-meteors/overview/ (accessed December 13, 2009).

NASA; Mission anniversary (accessed August 12, 2020).

Norris, R. n.d. "Where Aboriginals the World's First Astronomers?" https://atnf.csiro.au/people/rnorris/papers/a112.pdf (accessed February 28, 2020).

Ottewell, G. 1989. "The Earth as a Peppercorn." https://noao.edu/education/peppercorn/pcmain.html (accessed September 4, 2020).

Outdoor Lighting Basics. https://darksky.org/our-work/lighting/lighting-for-citizens/lighting-basics/ (accessed September 3, 2020).

Pogge, R. n.d. "An Introduction to Solar System Astronomy." http://astronomy.ohio-state.edu/~pogge/Ast161/Unit2/eclipses.html (accessed February 24, 2020).

Pogge, R. n.d. "An Introduction to Solar System Astronomy." http://astronomy.ohio-state.edu/~pogge/Ast161/Unit2/eclipses.html (accessed February 24, 2020).

Pöyry, V. n.d. "Top 5 Dreamiest Glass Igloos in Finland." https://herfinland.com/glass-igloos-finland/ (accessed February 26, 2020).

Pöyry, V. n.d. "TOP 5 Dreamiest Glass Igloos in Finland." https://herfinland.com/glass-igloos-finland/ (accessed February 26, 2020).

Pushkar, R.G. 2002. "Comet's Tale." Smithsonian Magazine, https://smithsonianmag.com/history/comets-tale-63573615 (accessed August 1, 2020).

Rao, J. 2013. "18th-Century Astronomer's Legacy Visible in Southern Night Sky." https://space.com/19919-southern-night-sky-constellations-lacaille.html (accessed October 24, 2020).

Rossiter, M. 2002. "Narrative and Stories in Adult Teaching and Learning Educational Resources Information Center 'ERIC Digest' (241)." https://eric.ed.gov/?id=ED473147 (accessed November 26, 2019).

Schneider, E. 2020. "Cecil SpacePort Snags Another Launch." https://bizjournals.com/jacksonville/news (accessed July 30, 2020).

Simkins, J.D. 2020. *Interest in Camping is at an All-Time High Following Covid 19 Outbreak*, Sunset Magazine, https://sunset.com/travel/wild-lands, (accessed August 25, 2020).

Source: statistica.com

Stephen, C. 2020. "Long March, Soyuz and Falcon Rockets Topped 2019's Launch Leaderboard." https://spaceflightnow.com (accessed November 25, 2020).

Stimac, V. 2019. "A Solar Eclipse is Coming this Summer. Here's Where to See It." https://nationalgeographic.com/travel/lists/where-to-see-2019-solar-eclipse-totality-partiality (accessed September 11, 2020).

Sumers, B. 2019. "Airlines Take Notice Of Millennials With New Strategies." https://skift.com/2019/05/09/ (accessed February 21, 2020).

The New World Atlas of Artificial Night Sky Brightness: https://advances.sciencemag.org/content/2/6/e1600377 (accessed January 31, 2020).

The Secrets of the Vatican Obelisk in St. Peter's Square. 2018. https://voxmundi.eu/secrets-vatican-obelisk/ (accessed August 24, 2020).

Thenumbers.com/movies/franchise/Star-Wars (accessed February 12, 2020).

Tips For Improving Night Vision https://rosecityastronomers.net/newsletter-content/2017/6/30/tips-for-improving-night-vision; (accessed August 31, 2020).

Turning off street lights does not lead to more crime or accidents—study. 2015. "The Guardian." https://theguardian.com/society/2015/jul/29/turning-off-street-lights-does-not-lead-to-more-or-accidents-study (accessed March 25, 2020).

UCSB ScienceLine, http://scienceline.ucsb.edu/getkey.php?key=923 (accessed September4, 2020).

Wall, M. 2017. "Great American Solar Eclipse Viewership Dwarfed Super Bowl Audience." https://space.com/38296 (accessed November 22, 2020).

Wall, M. 2020. "Virgin Galactic Unveils Sleek Interior of SpaceShipTwo Spaceliner." https://space.com/virgin-galactic-reveals-spaceshiptwo-interior.html(accessed August 19, 2020).

Williams, G. 1988. "Transformation: Critical Perspectives On Southern Africa." *Social Dynamics* 14, no. 1, 57–66, doi: 10.1080/02533958808458441 (accessed February 19, 2020).

Wilson, C. 2010. "Maxed Out: How Many Gs Can You Pull." https://newscientist.com/article/mg20627562 (accessed August 27, 2020).

Wood, T. 2020. "Who Owns Our Orbits." World Economic Forum https://weforum.org/agenda/2020/10/visualizing-easrth-satellites-sapce-spacex/ (accessed January 21, 2021).

Wood, T. 2020. "Who Owns Our Orbits; World Economic Forum." https://weforum.org/agenda/2020/10/visualizing-easrth-satellites-sapce-spacex/ (accessed January 21, 2021).

Resources: Organization and Phone Apps

Organizations

International Dark-Sky Association
International Astronomical Union
Starlight Foundation (Spain)
Royal Canadian Astronomical (Canada)
Astronomical Society of the Pacific (USA)
Campaign for Dark Skies (UK)
Cielo Buio (Italy)
ANPCEN (France)
Canadian Geographic (Canada)
Astronomitaly (Italy)

NASA (USA)
Consortium for Dark Sky Studies
International Occultation Timing Association
American Meteor Society

Star and Night Sky Apps

Star Chart [Android]
Star Walk [iOS]
Star Walk 2 [iOS]
Sky Safari 5 [iOS/Android]
Sky Safari 6 [iOS/Android]
Sky Safari 6AR [iOS/Android]
Sky Safari 6Plus [iOS/Android]
Sky Safari 6 Pro [iOS/Android]
Go Sky Watch [iOS/Android]
Triatlas [iOS]
Night Sky [iOS]
Star Chart [Android]
Sky View [iOS]
Sky Portal [Android]
Star Rover [Android]
Nasa App [iOS/Android]
Night Sky Lite [iOS/Android]
Star & Planet Finder [iOS]
ISS Detector [Android]
Star map [iOS]
Pocket Universe [iOS]
SkEye Astronomy [Android]
Deluxe Moon HD [iOS]
Sky Map [Android]
Solar Walk [iOS/Android]
Distance Suns [iOS/Android]
Stars Chart [iOS/Android}
Satellite Augmented Reality [Android]
Stellarium Plus [iOS/Android]

Sky Measuring Apps

Loss of the Night
Dark Sky Meter (iOS)
https://astrobackyard.com/the-bortle-scale/

Websites

earthsky.org
astrobackyard.com
www.starryskiesls.org
www.astroleague.org
cpdarkskies.org
darkskystudies.org
https://darkskies.vacations
spacetourismguide.com
shadowspro.com/en/world-sundials.html
www.UniversalWorkshop.com

Satellite Tracking Apps

Orbitrack

Eclipse Websites

https://timeanddate.com/eclipse/map/2024-april-8
www.eclipse-chasers.com
https://nationaleclipse.com/maps.html
https://eclipseguy.com
www.greatamericaneclipse.com
http://mreclipse.com/MrEclipse.html
https://sastrugipress.com/txeclipse
https://eclipse.gsfc.nasa.gov/eclipse.html
https://nationaleclipse.com
http://eclipsemegamovie.org
https://nationaleclipse.com
https://vimeo.com/73595112 (Animated video of flying with the shadow of
totality)

2024 Eclipse

https://eclipse2017.nasa.gov/safety
https://eclipse.aas.org/eclipse-america

Eclipse Safety Glasses

The American Astronomical Society has a comprehensive list of vendors who
make eclipse glasses and viewers that meet international safety standards that
can be found here:
https://eclipse.aas.org/resources/solar-filters

Campground Locators

http://onetuberadio.com/2017/06/29/eclipse-links

Product (Eclipse Glasses)

http://thousandoaksoptical.com/products/eclipse
https://rainbowsymphony.com
https://eclipseglasses.com
http://thousandoaksoptical.com/products/eclipse
https://luntsolarsystems.com/shop https://tse17.com

Tour Operators
https://aclassictour.com/solar-eclipse-tours
https://astro-eclipse.com
https://eclipsetraveler.com
https://tourradar.com
https://eclipsetours.com

Eclipse Videos
https://nasa.gov/eclipsevideos
https://space.com/33797-total-solar-eclipse-2017-guide.html
To know where to see the next Aurora go to:
https://services.swpc.noaa.gov/images/aurora-forecast-northern-hemisphere.jpg
To Get a 30-minute forecast here of the Aurora
https://swpc.noaa.gov/products/aurora-30-minute-forecast
http://aurora-service.net/ace-spacecraft

About the Author

Michael Marlin (aka Marlin) is a dark sky ambassador for the International Astronomical Union and International Dark-Sky Association. He is a public speaker on the issues and the solutions to light pollution for tourism boards, city councils, utility companies, educational institutions and science-centers. As a vanguard in the dark sky movement in the 80s, he created theatrical performances executed in the dark to raise awareness of our loss of night that played on five continents and across the United States. He is currently working on a television series where he will be hosting as "The Astrotourist."

Index

OTHER TITLES IN THE TOURISM AND HOSPITALITY MANAGEMENT COLLECTION

Betsy Bender Stringam, New Mexico State University, Editor

- *Food and Beverage Management in the Luxury Hotel Industry* by Sylvain Boussard
- *Targeting the Mature Traveler* by Jacqueline Jeynes
- *Hospitality* by Chris Sheppardson
- *Food and Architecture* by Subhadip Majumder, and Sounak Majumder
- *A Time of Change in Hospitality Leadership* by Chris Sheppardson
- *Improving Convention Center Management Using Business Analytics and Key Performance Indicators, Volume II* by Myles T. McGrane
- *Improving Convention Center Management Using Business Analytics and Key Performance Indicators , Volume I* by Myles T. McGrane
- *A Profile of the Hospitality Industry, Second Edition* by Betsy Bender Stringam
- *Cultural and Heritage Tourism and Management* by Tammie J. Kaufman
- *Marine Tourism, Climate Change, and Resilience in the Caribbean, Volume II* by Kreg Ettenger, Samantha Hogenson, and Martha Honey
- *Marketing Essentials for Independent Lodging* by Pamela Lanier
- *Marine Tourism, Climate Change, and Resiliency in the Caribbean, Volume I* by Samantha Hogenson, and Martha Honey
- *Catering and Convention Service Survival Guide in Hotels and Casinos* by Lisa Lynn Backus, and Patti J. Shock,

Announcing the Business Expert Press Digital Library

Concise e-books business students need for classroom and research

This book can also be purchased in an e-book collection by your library as

- a one-time purchase,
- that is owned forever,
- allows for simultaneous readers,
- has no restrictions on printing, and
- can be downloaded as PDFs from within the library community.

Our digital library collections are a great solution to beat the rising cost of textbooks. E-books can be loaded into their course management systems or onto students' e-book readers.
The **Business Expert Press** digital libraries are very affordable, with no obligation to buy in future years. For more information, please visit **www.businessexpertpress.com/librarians**. To set up a trial in the United States, please email **sales@businessexpertpress.com**.